THE TWENTIETH CENTURY WORLD
War, revolution and technology

Sean Lang
Head of History
Hills Road Sixth Form College,
Cambridge

CAMBRIDGE
UNIVERSITY PRESS

PUBLISHED BY THE PRESS SYNDICATE OF THE UNIVERSITY OF CAMBRIDGE
The Pitt Building, Trumpington Street, Cambridge CB2 1RP, United Kingdom

CAMBRIDGE UNIVERSITY PRESS
The Edinburgh Building, Cambridge CB2 2RU, United Kingdom
40 West 20th Street, New York, NY 10011-4211, USA
10 Stamford Road, Oakleigh, Melbourne 3166, Australia

First published 1998

Printed in the United Kingdom at the University Press, Cambridge

Typeset in Times Roman

A catalogue record for this book is available from the British Library

ISBN 0 521 48324 7 paperback
Designed and produced by Gecko Limited, Bicester, Oxon.
Illustrations by Nick Asher, Barry Rowe, Martin Sanders and Mel Wright
Picture research by Marilyn Rawlings

> **Notice to teachers**
> Many of the sources used in this textbook have been adapted or abridged from the original.

Acknowledgements

The author and publisher would like to thank the following for permission to use illustrations:

The Advertising Archives, pages 42 right and 128 left; AKG London, pages 27 left, 134 centre left, 142 inset left, 154 above, 158 above and below left; Archiv für Kunst und Geschichte, Berlin, 67; Bildarchiv Preussischer Kulturbesitz, pages 4 inset below, 16 inset, 30–1, 51 left, 80 top (Arthur Grimm), 98 (Richard Peter, 1946) and 155; Bilderdienst Süddeutscher Verlag, pages 15, 39 right, 56 inset below, 133 below and 134 below left; Bridgeman Art Library, pages 14 (Imperial War Museum) and 37; Camera Press, pages 13 inset below (Imperial War Museum), 66, 122, 124–5 and inset, 136 above right, 144 left, 148 below left (Zimmerman/Curtis), 149 above and 151; Corbis-Bettmann, pages 126 inset (UPI), 127 inset (Reuter), 129 left (UPI), 135 below (UPI), 136 below right, 138 (UPI) and 154 below (UPI); D-Day Museum, Portsmouth, 102–3 bottom (Panel 34 of the Overlord Embroidery, on permanent display at the museum); ET Archive, pages 12–13, 18 right (Imperial War Museum), 20–1 (Imperial War Museum), 50 and 120 right; Mary Evans Picture Library, pages 4–5, 38 above centre and 76; Ronald Grant Archive, page 47 below; Hulton Getty, pages 8, 41, 42 above left and below left, 47 above right, 48 right, 53, 121 right, 129 right, 146 left and right; Robert Hunt Library, 61 bottom, 80 bottom (John Heseltine), 81 top (Novosti), 105 top (Novosti); Imperial War Museum, pages 23, 55, 59, 64 inset, 69 insets, 70 top, 71, 73 below, 74 left, 77, 89 bottom, 93 inset, 95, 108 inset and 109 inset; David King Collection, pages 24 left, 26, 27 right, 28, 29, 30 inset, 34, 35 above and below, 36 above and below; Magnum Photos, pages 119 (Cartier-Bresson), 123 above (Burri), 126–7 (Imaeda), 135 above (Lessing) and 148–9 (Steele Perkins); Peter Newark's Historical Pictures, pages 4 insets above left and above right, 5 inset above, 16–17, 19, 20 inset, 29 inset, 38–9 above, 44, 45, 46, 47 above left, 48 left, 61 top, 68–9 background, 72 right, 75, 79, 96 (Roy Nockolds), 105 bottom, 106, 116–17, 124 inset above left, 130 right, 132, 133 centre, 140 and 142 inset right; Novosti Photo Library, London, 81 bottom; Popperfoto, pages 5 inset below, 13 inset above, 21 inset, 25 right, 38 left, 38–9 below, 40, 49, 58, 62, 65 inset, 72 left, 73 top, 94 top, 100, 111, 113 inset, 128 right, 131, 144 right, 145, 148 above left, 152–3, 158–9 and 159 above right; Rex Features, pages 88, 90 and 136 left; Sygma, 104 (© Keystone); Topham Picturepoint, pages 10, 22, 24–5, 25 above left, 43, 54, 63 below, 70 centre, 89 top, 92 top, 94 bottom, 120 left, 121 left, 123 below, 128 centre, 130 left, 141, 142–3, 147, 149 below right, 156 and 157 above; TRH/NASM, 97 top; TRH/DOD, 110; Ullstein Bilderdienst, pages 18 left, 51 right, 52, 56 inset above, 112–13, 117, 118 inset, 134 above right, 137 and 157 below; Universal Pictorial Press, page 139; USAF/ Ann Ronan at Image Select, 108–9 background; Wiener Library, pages 63 top, 74 right and 92–3 background (© The Auschwitz Museum).

The front cover illustration *Ruby Loftus Screwing a Breech-ring* was painted by Dame Laura Knight during the Second World War and shows women manufacturing war supplies (Imperial War Museum).

CONTENTS

INTRODUCTION: THE WORLD IN 1900

What was the world like in 1900?

Monarchies

In 1900 most of the world was dominated by the rulers of Europe. Many of these rulers were related to each other. Kaiser Wilhelm II of Germany and Tsar Nicholas II of Russia were cousins. King Edward VII of Great Britain was their uncle.

Empires

Vast areas of Africa and Asia had been colonised by Europeans. Europeans obtained raw materials for industries from these colonies but they also built railways and schools for the people they ruled. These empires made Europe rich, but they also caused the European countries to be suspicious of each other.

Class

Europe in 1900 was divided by class. The upper class owned the land; the middle class controlled industry or ran shops and offices; the working class worked in factories or in the fields. They also worked as servants for richer people. Many working-class people lived in dreadful poverty.

King Edward VII.

Kaiser Wilhelm II.

Tsar Nicholas II.

Railways and motor cars

In 1900 it was possible to travel across Europe, America or Africa by train. The first motor cars had recently been developed. Within a few years, the Model T Ford was produced, which was cheap enough for many people to buy.

Air and sea travel

The American brothers, Wilbur and Orville Wright, were the first to fly a few hundred metres in an aeroplane in 1903. Within six years, the Frenchman Louis Blériot was to fly across the English Channel. At sea, great luxury ocean liners competed to cross the Atlantic in the fastest time.

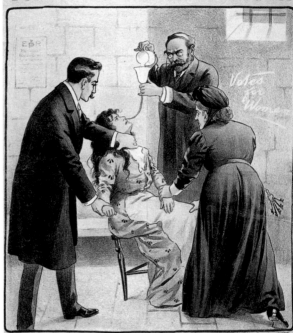

Suffragettes were often arrested and sent to prison. This poster shows a suffragette being force-fed by prison guards, while on hunger strike.

Medicine

In medicine, the bacillus that causes tuberculosis (TB) had been discovered, and more people were being vaccinated against smallpox. Pierre and Marie Curie had worked on developing X-rays. But many people still died when ordinary wounds became infected.

Marie Curie at her microscope.

Votes for women!

In 1900, no woman, anywhere in the world, had the right to vote. Norwegian women were to win the vote in 1913. In Britain, suffragettes led by Mrs Emmeline Pankhurst often staged violent demonstrations demanding the vote.

Revolutionaries

There were many revolutionary groups in Europe who wanted to bring down governments by force. Russian revolutionaries had already blown up Tsar Alexander II in 1881, and in 1911 they shot the Russian prime minister. In 1914, a Bosnian revolutionary was to assassinate the son of the Austrian Emperor in Sarajevo. This act sparked off the First World War.

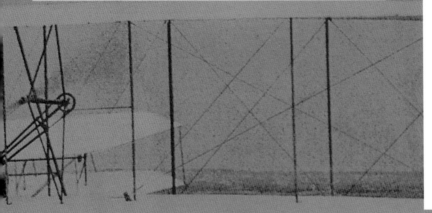

Wilbur and Orville Wright's aeroplane.

1914: The outbreak of war

After the Archduke Franz Ferdinand was assass-inated in Bosnia, Austria-Hungary declared war on Serbia. Tied by their alliances, other countries quickly joined in. Russia and France supported Serbia; Germany supported Austria-Hungary. When German troops invaded Belgium, Britain declared war on Germany.

1914: Tannenberg and the Marne

In the first few months of the war, the Germans surrounded and crushed a huge Russian army at Tannenberg. In the west, German troops swept through Belgium towards Paris. The Paris garrison left the city and stopped the Germans at the River Marne. After that, the sides fought each other from two lines of trenches.

1915: Gallipoli

Turkey supported Germany. In 1915, Australian, New Zealand and British troops attacked her at Gallipoli but they were pinned down on the coast and had to with-draw. The British also helped the Arabs rise up against Turkish rule in the Middle East.

1916: Verdun and the Somme

The Germans and French became involved in a desper-ate and bloody battle at Verdun. The British launched their own attack on the Germans near the River Somme, but it went disastrously wrong. On the first day alone, the British lost 60,000 men.

WORLD WAR

1916: Jutland

In a naval battle in 1916, off Jutland, in Denmark, the British lost more ships than the Germans, but the German fleet returned to port and never went to sea again. After this, the Germans relied on attacks by U-boats (submarines).

1917: America goes to war; Revolution in Russia

Exasperated by German U-boat attacks on her ships, the USA declared war on Germany in April 1917. In the meantime, revolution broke out in Russia and Vladimir Ilyich Lenin's new Bolshevik government made peace with Germany.

1918: Breakthrough in the West

In 1917 the British tried to break through the German lines at Passchendaele, in Belgium, but they got hopelessly stranded in the appalling mud. In 1918 a German attack broke through the British lines, but was finally driven back with massive American help.

1918: Armistice

Exhausted by the war, the German people rebelled and overthrew the Kaiser. The new German government signed an armistice (cease-fire) with the Allies. Germany surrendered and the war was over.

1 The outbreak of the First World War

The war began when the heir to the Austrian-Hungarian Empire was shot dead by a Bosnian Serb, in Sarajevo, in 1914.

Why did a quarrel between the Austrians and the Serbs cause a world war?

Austria and Serbia

Bosnia has a mixed population, which includes many Serbs. In 1908, the Austrians marched into Bosnia. The Bosnian Serbs wanted them to leave. In June 1914, the heir to the Austrian throne, Archduke Franz Ferdinand and his wife were visiting the Bosnian capital, Sarajevo. A group of Bosnian terrorists, the Black Hand, gunned them down. The assassin was a schoolboy called Gavrilo Princip; his gun came from Serbia.

The Austrian government decided the time had come to crush Serbia once and for all.

War

The Austrians demanded that Serbia should apologise for the Archduke's murder and allow the Austrian police into Serbia to hunt down the culprits; Serbia had forty-eight hours to agree or there would be war.

The Serbs offered to help find the assassins but Austria was not satisfied. On 28 July 1914, Austria-Hungary declared war on Serbia. Both sides turned to their allies for help.

Source A

Archduke Ferdinand and his wife during their visit to Sarajevo in 1914.

Alliances

An alliance is an agreement between countries to help if one of them is attacked. The map shows how the European countries were allied to each other. In 1914, each side declared war on the other.

All these great powers brought their empires into the war with them. British territories like India, South Africa, Canada and the British West Indies sent troops to Europe, and so did French colonies like Senegal and Algeria. Although the war began in Europe, it was a world war from the start.

Source B

A senior British official thought the quarrel between Austria and Serbia was not the real reason war started:

'This struggle … is not for the possession of Serbia, but one between Germany aiming at a political dictatorship in Europe, and the Powers who desire to retain individual freedom.'

Sir Eyre Crowe, 1914

Declarations of war

1914

28 July	Austria declares war on Serbia
30 July	Russia calls up her troops to help Serbia
31 July	Germany tells Russia to disband her troops
1 August	Germany declares war on Russia France calls up her troops
3 August	Germany declares war on France Great Britain warns Germany not to invade Belgium
4 August	Germany invades Belgium Great Britain declares war on Germany

---

1 Why did the Black Hand kill Archduke Ferdinand?

2 Look at the map carefully. Using the map and other information in this unit, explain in your own words how the assassination led to a European war.

Alliances between the Great Powers in 1914.

2 War in the trenches

Both sides were expecting a short war in 1914; instead the conflict soon got down bogged down in a stalemate and the appalling slaughter of trench warfare.

What went wrong?

The Schlieffen Plan

In 1914, the Germans had a plan to defeat the French quickly with a rapid knock-out attack. It was named the Schlieffen Plan, after the war minister who designed it.

The French army stopped the German attack at the Battle of the Marne and so saved Paris. Neither side could get past the other, so they dug themselves in. The line of trenches stretched from the Swiss border to the sea.

British and Belgian troops hold up the German advance at Mons. They then fall back to the River Marne.

German troops advance to the border by train.

Behind schedule, the Germans turn south.

French and British troops attack the Germans who are held at the River Marne.

HOLLAND

Antwerp

BELGIUM

Brussels

Mons

R.Somme

LUXEMBOURG

Lorraine

GERMANY

R.Seine

Paris

R.Marne

FRANCE

SWITZERL

The Schlieffen Plan in action.

The soldiers lived and slept in underground dugouts

10

Trench warfare

Trench warfare resulted from the threat of the machine gun. A single gun could cut down huge numbers of men, so they were forced to take refuge from the danger of enemy machine guns in trenches. After the autumn and winter rains, these soon became waterlogged. The mud was so thick that men could drown in it.

Source A

An officer in the Devonshire Regiment described life in the trenches.

'The conditions were terrible. Imagine the agony of a fellow standing for twenty-four hours, sometimes to his waist in mud … Many men got trench feet and trench fever. With trench fever a fellow had a very high temperature and constant diarrhoea. It left him weak and listless. Trench feet was owing to the wet sogging through your boots. In many cases your toes nearly rotted off in your boots. We lost more that way than we did from wounds.'

Captain Ulick Burke, 1917

KEY

Original Schlieffen Plan by which Germans hoped to encircle Paris

Actual route of German troops

Direction taken by French troops

Periscope

Barbed wire

No-man's-land

Machine gun

Parapet

A bank of earth called the parados gave the soldiers some protection from behind

Fire step

Duck boards

A German trench. The Germans dug their trenches much deeper than the British and French.

11

The Battle of the Somme: 1916

The generals on both sides tried to think of ways to break through the enemy trenches. In 1915, the Germans began to use poison gas. The British and French were horrified, but soon used it themselves. The gas choked men to death or left them blinded, but it failed to break the deadlock. In 1916, the Germans launched a full-scale attack on the French fort of Verdun. This battle was so fierce that the British had to launch their own attack to relieve the pressure on the French. The British General, Haig, decided to try to break through the German trenches near the River Somme.

Haig's plan was simple. He ordered a week-long artillery barrage that he hoped would cut the German barbed wire and flatten their trenches. After this, British soldiers would advance across no-man's-land and capture the German trenches. The British cavalry would then be able to charge through the German lines.

The attack, scheduled for 1 July 1916, was a disaster. The artillery barrage could even be heard in London but the Germans were able to shelter in their deep dug-outs and wait for the shelling to stop. When the British soldiers began to advance on foot across no-man's-land they were easy targets for the German machine gunners.

The advancing troops also became hopelessly bogged down in the mud. When the fighting stopped in November, 1 million men had been killed or injured. When another French attack collapsed in 1917, with casualties of over 100,000 men, some French soldiers mutinied.

Source B

A painting of the battlefield at the Somme by André Devambez.

Source C

Canadian machine gunners sheltering in a shell hole during the Battle of Passchendaele in 1917.

Tanks

The British first used tanks against the German trenches in the Battle of the Somme, but most broke down. A larger number of British tanks finally broke through the German trenches at the Battle of Cambrai in 1917, but it was found that they went too fast for the British infantry to keep up. Many tanks were captured when they stopped after developing engine trouble.

Source D

Tanks carried a bundle of sticks, called a fascine, that could be dropped into shell holes to allow the tank to cross. Even so, this tank has become stuck in deep mud during the fighting at Cambrai. You can clearly see its machine guns and the caterpillar tracks that allow it to cross muddy ground more easily.

War with Turkey

Turkey fought on the German side in the war. In 1915, the Allies landed troops in Turkey, at Gallipoli. Many of the troops came from the Australian and New Zealand Army Corps (Anzac). The Turks fought back so fiercely that the Allies had to dig in on the beaches, and then found it hard to advance very far inland. After eight months, it was decided to withdraw and sail home.

In 1914, the Turks ruled over a large empire which included the Middle East. In 1916, the Arabs, led by Sherif Hussein of Mecca, revolted against the Turks, helped by a British officer, T. E. Lawrence (Lawrence of Arabia). The British and the Arabs drove the Turks out of Palestine and Syria.

1917: America joins in

At first the USA kept out of the war, even after the Germans sank the passenger liner, *Lusitania*, killing over a thousand people, including 124 Americans. But, in 1917, the Americans learned that the Germans were encouraging Mexico to attack the USA. On 2 April 1917 the USA declared war on Germany. Thousands of fresh American troops were sent to help the French and British repel the last German attacks in 1918.

Source E

A painting by Charles Dixon of the Anzac troops landing in the Gallipoli peninsula.

Source F

Russian troops captured during the Brusilov offensive. This was very successful at first but, eventually, Brusilov's advance was stopped by the Germans and thousands of Russians were taken prisoner.

Breakthrough

In 1916, the Russian General Brusilov had shown that it was possible to break through the trenches. He simply attacked the Austrians without any previous artillery bombardment and caught them by surprise. In March 1918, the Germans did the same to the British. The British line broke and the Germans rushed on towards Paris. By then, American troops had begun to arrive in France. Together with the Americans, the French and British stopped the German advance and broke through the German lines in several places. On 11 November 1918, the Germans realised they were defeated and asked for peace.

---

1 Look carefully at the diagram on page 10. Explain in your own words how the Schlieffen Plan should have worked. Why do you think it failed?

2 Look at the drawing of the trench. List at least three advantages the men in the trenches had over anyone attacking them.

3 Why did the attack on the Somme fail?

4 The generals on each side tried many different ways to break through the trenches. Find at least *four* in this unit, and say why each failed.

3 The war at sea and in the air

Before 1914, Germany invested vast sums in a huge fleet and built a number of airships.
How far did these preparations really affect the course of the war?

Dreadnoughts

In 1903, an Italian journalist suggested that it should be possible to design a battleship with thicker armour plating, heavier guns, and more of them, than anyone had thought possible. Within three years, the British had launched the world's first super-battleship, HMS *Dreadnought*. The Germans quickly copied the design.

Blockade and raiders

The dreadnoughts' main role was to attack enemy merchant shipping, and so stop food and war supplies getting through. One German raider, the *Emden*, sank or captured 25 Allied ships before it was sunk. The British blockaded Germany's ports, to stop her bringing in any food. British and German dreadnoughts also fought each other. In November 1914, the German Admiral, Graf Spee, sank several British warships off the Chilean coast at Coronel. In December, the British were able to sink most of his fleet near the Falkland Islands.

U-boats

The Germans also used submarines called U-boats (Unterseeboote) to attack Allied shipping. U-boats also attacked passenger ships, like the *Lusitania*, if they suspected them of carrying war supplies.

Source A

A painting of a German U-boat on the surface, after sinking an Allied merchant ship.

The Battle of Jutland

In 1916, the German admiral, Scheer, sent out a small force of ships to lead the British Grand Fleet into a trap.

At first the plan worked. The British admiral, Sir David Beatty, chased Scheer's ships, but then found himself outnumbered by more powerful German ships. But the British commander, Sir John Jellicoe, steamed to Beatty's rescue with a large force of dreadnoughts. Scheer fired torpedoes at Jellicoe's ships and turned for home. The British lost 14 ships at Jutland, and the Germans lost 11. The Germans returned to port and never ventured out again.

The effects of the blockade

The British blockade forced the Germans to ration bread and other foods. By the end of 1916, food was so short that the winter became known as the 'turnip winter' because that was about all there was to eat. The blockade helped convince the Germans that they should make peace.

Source B

A painting of the Battle of Jutland by Winston McGovan.

Aircraft and Zeppelins

At first, both sides photographed enemy trenches from aeroplanes. Soon pilots started shooting pistols and rifles at each other in the air. After a Dutch engineer, Anthony Fokker, worked out a system by which machine gun bullets could be made to miss the rotating propeller blades, each side set out to shoot the enemy down. Many successful fighter pilots, like the Red Baron, the German Baron Manfred von Richthofen, with his red aeroplanes, became very famous.

Zeppelins

The Germans had also developed very large airships, called Zeppelins after their inventor, Count Zeppelin. In 1915, the first Zeppelins started bombing British towns and factories.

The Zeppelins could create enormous damage. One raid destroyed half-a-million pounds' worth of property. Angry mobs attacked shops with foreign-sounding names. Anti-aircraft guns could not shoot high enough to harm the airships but, in 1916, British aircraft were equipped with incendiary bullets. These were able to set light to the gas inside the Zeppelins' balloons.

Source C

A London house damaged by bombs dropped during a Zeppelin raid.

Source D

A painting by Gordon Crosby of a Zeppelin on fire after being shot at by a British fighter pilot.

---

1 What did each side use its dreadnoughts for? How useful were they?

2 Who won the Battle of Jutland? (Think carefully about this.)

3 Which do you think proved more effective: the Zeppelin attacks on Britain or the Allied blockade of Germany?

4 The Home Front

The First World War directly affected civilians at home and some of the changes that came about would be very important after the war.

How deeply did the war change civilian life?

Recruitment

When, in August 1914, the war began, young men on both sides rushed to join the army. Everyone assumed the war would be over by Christmas. But once trench warfare started and casualties became heavy, both sides became short of men. In 1916, Britain introduced conscription. Any young man could be called up to serve in the armed forces.

Conscientious objectors

Not everyone agreed with the war. People who objected to fighting were known as conscientious objectors. They were generally very unpopular, and nicknamed 'conchies'. Some of them were prepared to serve as ambulance drivers or stretcher-bearers, but others refused to have anything to do with war at all.

Source A

A British recruiting poster showing the popular hero, the British General, Lord Kitchener.

Source B

A soldier, Private A. E. Hollingshead, recalls how he was able to enlist.

'I was only fifteen and every time I tried to join up in London it was no good, they wouldn't have me. So I went by rail to Birmingham, on a penny platform ticket. I went into a recruiting office there and told them I was seventeen. The sergeant said, 'Why don't you go out and have something to eat? When you come back you might be a bit older'. I told him I had no money and he gave me two bob. When I came back he spoke to me as though he had never seen me before. I said I was eighteen and, this time, I got in all right.'

Martin Middlebrook, *The First Day on the Somme*, 1984

Source C

A conscientious objector explains to a military tribunal why he cannot serve in a military ambulance unit.

'To me, war is murder, murder in the mass. It is a crime, the greatest crime. I make no charge against other men. Most soldiers are following their consciences and I admire their courage ... I have refused service as an officer telegraphist in the Signal section of the Royal Engineers. I cannot assist others in the destruction of that which I hold sacred. I should be a coward if I assisted in passing on the ammunition which I could not use myself.'

James Jesson French, 7 August 1916

19

Women at war

With so many men being called up to fight, women had to keep the factories and farms going. Before the war, some women had been demonstrating for the right to vote. Now, many of these suffragettes volunteered for war work, and soon showed they could work lathes or drive buses just as well as men.

Some 900,000 British women worked in munitions factories filling shells with explosives. They became known as 'canaries', because the explosives stained their clothes, skin and hair bright yellow. It was dangerous work, and more than 300 women were killed in explosions or accidents. There were severe penalties for breaking the safety regulations. A woman who was found with even a single match in her pocket could be arrested for attempted sabotage.

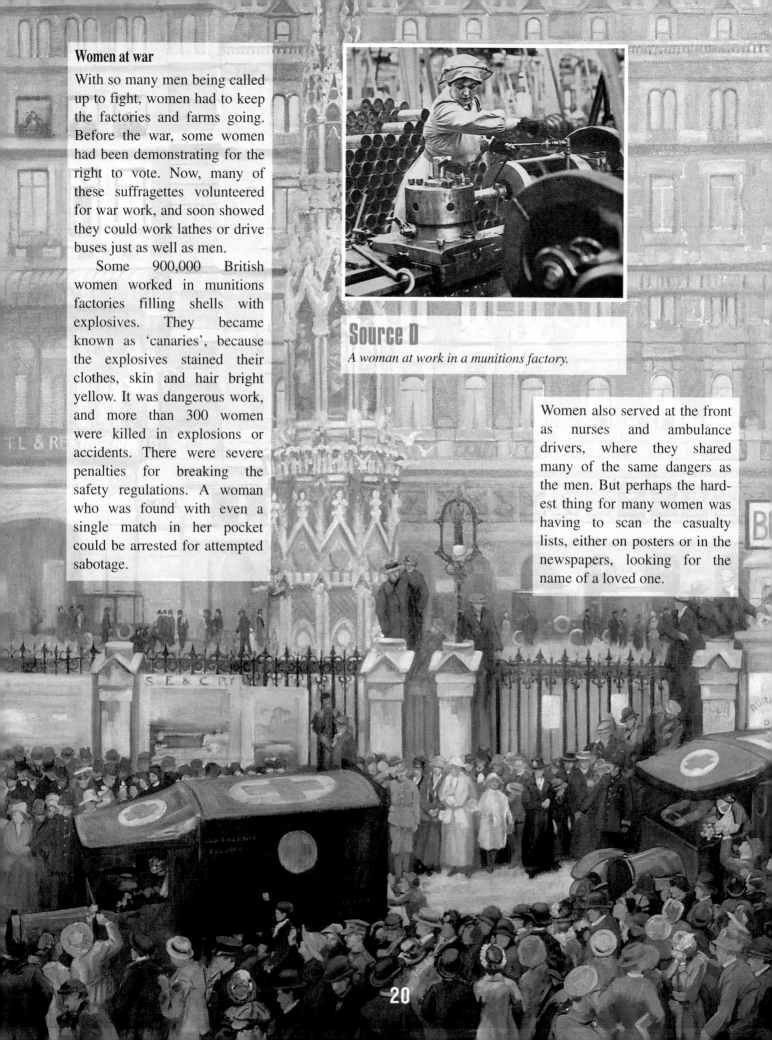

Source D
A woman at work in a munitions factory.

Women also served at the front as nurses and ambulance drivers, where they shared many of the same dangers as the men. But perhaps the hardest thing for many women was having to scan the casualty lists, either on posters or in the newspapers, looking for the name of a loved one.

Food and drink

As Britain imported much of her food from abroad, the German U-boat campaign hit directly at Britain's food supply. At first this only meant that prices went up but, as the war went on, some foodstuffs became very scarce. The government encouraged people to grow their own vegetables. Many modern allotments date from the First World War. By 1918, supplies of meat were so short that cafés and restaurants were told to have two 'meatless' days every week.

Source F

A grocer's shop, closed because of lack of food supplies.

In 1917, the first cases of influenza caused by a deadly new strain of virus appeared in Spain. It spread rapidly across Europe, killing thousands of people weakened by hunger and hardship caused by the war.

Source E

A painting, by J. Hodgson Lobley, showing casualties from the Battle of the Somme arriving at Charing Cross station in July 1916.

1 How is the poster in Source A designed to work?

2 Write a diary for a woman on the Home Front in Britain.

3 If you were a German spy in Britain, would you report that the war was popular or unpopular with ordinary British people? Use all the evidence in this unit to help you answer.

5 The Treaty of Versailles

In June 1919, the victorious Allies signed the Treaty of Versailles. Between them, they were to decide the future of Europe.

How was Germany treated by the victors?

The Armistice

In 1918, after the massive German attack in the west failed, the German people, tired of war, overthrew the Kaiser. The new German government asked for a cease-fire or armistice. The fighting stopped at 11.00 a.m. on 11 November 1918.

Earlier in 1918, US President Wilson had published 14 points he believed any peace settlement should include, if the world was to be kept safe for democracy. One key point was national self-determination – allowing people to rule themselves. The German government was encouraged by this and expected fair treatment from the victorious Allies.

Crowds celebrated in the streets in Britain and France but, amongst all the celebrations, there were calls to punish the Germans severely for the war. The British Prime Minister, David Lloyd George, promised to 'squeeze Germany till the pips squeak'.

The terms of the treaty

● Germany loses lands
In 1919 the Allied leaders met in Paris to draw up a peace settlement. The Germans were not invited. Wilson, Lloyd George and the French Prime Minister, Clemenceau, decided that Germany should give up land in Europe to her neighbours – France, Belgium, Denmark and Poland – and that all German overseas colonies should be taken over by the Allies.

● Army reductions
It was also decided that Germany's army should be cut down to 100,000 men. German tanks were to be destroyed and the airforce disbanded. The German fleet sailed to Scotland and sunk itself rather than surrender to the Allies.

● Reparations and war guilt
The final treaty was signed at Versailles. It blamed the Germans for starting the war, and forced them to pay reparations (damages) to the other powers. The Germans felt very bitter about this diktat (dictated peace) but they had no choice but to sign it.

Source A *Crowds celebrating on Armistice night.*

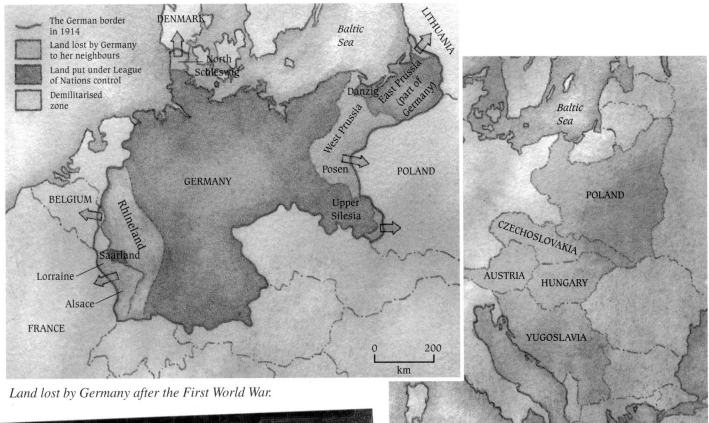

Land lost by Germany after the First World War.

New states created in 1919.

Source B

Source B

The signing of the Treaty of Versailles.

New states in Central Europe

In 1919 other treaties dealt with Austria-Hungary, Bulgaria and Turkey. The Austro-Hungarian Empire was broken up and the new 'successor states' of Austria, Hungary, Poland and Czechoslovakia were created in its place.

The League of Nations

The Allies set up a League of Nations to try to solve problems through discussion, hoping to avoid future wars. But neither the Germans nor the Russians were allowed to join and the American government refused to take part. The League had no armed forces of its own and found it difficult to solve the problems of the following years.

---

1 Explain why many Germans were so bitter about the Treaty of Versailles.

2 Why do you think the Allies were so anxious to punish Germany for the war?

23

6 The Russian Revolution

Towards the end of the First World War communist revolutionaries, known as Bolsheviks, seized power in Russia. This was one of the most significant events in the history of the twentieth century.

Why did Russia collapse in revolution in 1917?

In 1900, the vast Russian Empire stretched from Poland in the west through central Asia, beyond Mongolia and China, reaching nearly to Alaska. It contained people of many nationalities other than Russian. They spoke different languages, followed different religions, and even used different alphabets, but almost everyone lived in the countryside, in utter poverty. The peasants still worked for their local lords in the same way as they had done since medieval times.

Source B

An English visitor describes a visit to a great Russian estate in 1909.

'We went home followed by over 2,000 peasants from the Estate. For a whole 1½ hours the Princess stood and heard the welcomes and complaints from various tenants ... It was interesting to see the peasants talking to the Princess. The men were very respectful and the women were very frightened and inclined to cry. Many of them prefaced their requests by kneeling down to kiss the ground on which the Princess was standing.'

A Summer Vacation with Prince Yousopoff in University College Record, 1982

Source A

Russian peasants working in the fields in 1900.

Source C

Peasant women hauling a raft upstream in 1910.

Although most of Russia was agricultural, there were two major industrial cities, Moscow and St Petersburg, the capital. The factory workers in these cities lived in appalling slums, with most lacking running water or sanitation. Each year, thousands died of disease or malnutrition.

Source D
Russian workers in the slums.

Source E
The Tsar and Tsarina with their five children photographed aboard their yacht.

Nicholas II

In 1900, Russia was ruled by an all-powerful emperor, Tsar Nicholas II. There was no parliament, no elections, and although the Tsar had ministers, he did not have to listen to them. Nicholas himself was a kindly man, with a large family whom he loved dearly, but he was dominated by his German wife, the Tsarina Alexandra. He hated change, and Alexandra encouraged him to stand firm against those who wanted it.

Bloody Sunday

In 1904, Russia went to war with Japan, and to the Russians' surprise and anger, the Japanese won easily. In 1905, the crew of the battleship *Potemkin* mutinied and took over the ship. In St Petersburg, a huge crowd of working people led by a priest, Father Gapon, marched to the Tsar's Winter Palace to ask him to help them buy bread. They found their way blocked by troops who opened fire, killing hundreds. The day became known as Bloody Sunday.

To end the crisis of 1905, Nicholas II gave the Russians a parliament with limited powers called the Duma. Despite this, the Russian people would never trust him again.

Source F

A painting of the events of Bloody Sunday.

Revolutionaries

There were many groups who wanted to overthrow the Tsar. The most important were the communists, who followed the ideas of the German writer, Karl Marx. Marx said that all industrial countries were bound to have a revolution where the workers would take control of the government and of all factories and mines.

But, apart from Moscow and St Petersburg, Russia was not an industrial country. The Russian communists could not decide how important this was and split into two different groups with different attitudes: the Mensheviks and the Bolsheviks.

The Mensheviks believed that Russia should industrialise first before staging a revolution. The Bolsheviks, led by Vladimir Ilyich Lenin, believed that Russia should have a revolution immediately.

Source G

A portrait, painted in 1924, showing Lenin addressing a crowd of supporters.

The first revolution: March 1917

In 1914, Russia went to war against Germany and Austria. The First World War was a disaster for Russia. The Germans defeated her armies, and took thousands of prisoners. The Tsar took command of the army, but this just meant that he was blamed when things went wrong. Russian soldiers started to disobey orders and go home. In March 1917, the workers in St Petersburg went on strike. When Nicholas ordered his soldiers to deal with the strikers, they refused. Without anyone planning it, the Russian Revolution had begun.

Rasputin

Tsarina Alexandra had fallen under the influence of Rasputin, a mysterious, hypnotic holy man who seemed able to help her son's haemophilia (a disease where the blood fails to clot). Although he knew nothing of politics, she allowed him to influence the government while Tsar Nicholas was in charge of the Russian army at the front.

Source H

Rasputin.

27

The second revolution: November 1917

Once his soldiers started refusing to obey him, Nicholas had no choice but to abdicate. He and his family were arrested by the new government, led by Alexander Kerensky. Kerensky wanted to hold free elections and, until then, his government was provisional (temporary). But he also decided that Russia would stay in the war against Germany. This was a fatal mistake.

The war continued to go badly and food shortages at home got worse. By the autumn, the Provisional Government was as unpopular as the Tsar had been. Lenin and his fellow Bolshevik leader, Leon Trotsky, drew up plans for a second revolution. Soldiers and volunteers flocked to Trotsky's headquarters; Kerensky had only a few officer cadets to defend his headquarters, the Winter Palace. On the night of 7 November, the Bolsheviks attacked.

Source I

An artist's impression, painted some time after the event, of the storming of the Winter Palace.

It was not much of a battle. The warship *Aurora* fired two shells; the Bolsheviks fired a number of bullets that hit five of their own men; and a few Bolsheviks slipped through a side door and arrested the Provisional Government. Kerensky had already left.

Source J

Trotsky describes the attack on the Winter Palace.

'The attack on the palace was opened by a few blank rounds being fired from the fortress as a preliminary warning. This was followed by a massed onslaught from both sides, armoured cars and machine guns firing at the palace from under the archway on the square, while now and then the guns of the fortress or of the cruiser *Aurora* thundered and crashed above the din. Actually, however, a good many of the shots were only gun-cotton, and the firing in all cases was so inaccurate that the palace was only hit three times from the river.'

L. D. Trotsky, *History of the Russian Revolution*

Source K

Lenin delivering a speech in a Moscow square in 1918. Trotsky is standing on the right of the platform.

Lenin in power

Lenin had been in Switzerland when the March revolution broke out. The Germans smuggled him into Russia so that he could overthrow the Provisional Government. Kerensky issued a warrant for his arrest so he had to go into hiding again. He had returned to St Petersburg just in time for the attack on the Winter Palace in November.

Lenin told the Russians that he offered them 'Peace! Bread! Land!'. In order to fulfil this promise he took complete power. He set up a new secret police force, the *Cheka*, and immediately closed down the newly elected Russian Parliament.

He decided to make peace with the Germans at any price. In 1918, the Treaty of Brest-Litovsk handed large areas of Russia over to the Germans.

He also handed over all lands belonging to the Church and the nobles to the peasants.

Source L

Trotsky reviewing the Red Army troops.

Civil War

Between 1918 and 1921, there was a civil war in Russia between the Reds and the Whites. The Bolsheviks were known as the Reds because of their red flags. Those who opposed them were called the Whites, though, in fact, not all Whites had the same motives for joining in the Civil War. Some were Royalists who wanted to restore the Tsar but others were nationalist non-Russians who wanted to take the opportunity to pull out of Russia. Allied troops from Britain, France, the USA and Japan also intervened in the Civil War to help the Whites defeat the Reds. The peasants now owned the land they farmed, and they did not want anyone to take it from them. But both sides seized their crops and forced the peasants to join them. Peasants, therefore, would often fight for whichever army they happened to encounter first.

Source M
A group of Red Army soldiers during the Civil War.

Source N
A poster issued during the Civil War urging the Reds to defend the Revolution.

War Communism

The Red Army was led by Leon Trotsky. Trotsky took advantage of the divisions among the Whites to defeat them one by one. To feed his men, Trotsky simply seized whatever he needed. Thousands of Russian peasants were left to starve. Some even turned to cannibalism.

Trotsky and Lenin called these ruthless methods 'War Communism' and said they were necessary to win the war. When the sailors at the Kronstadt naval base staged a mutiny in protest at War Communism, Trotsky moved the Red Army in and crushed them without mercy. War Communism worked. Trotsky won the Civil War, and Lenin was now free to turn Russia into the world's first communist state.

The New Economic Policy

It was only in 1921, after the Civil War, that Lenin announced a New Economic Policy (NEP). Under it the peasants no longer had their produce confiscated by the state and all Russians, including the peasants, could even sell a limited amount of their produce for profit.

1 How many reasons can you find to explain why the Russians overthrew the Tsar in March 1917?

2 Why did Lenin and Trotsky stage a second revolution to overthrow the Provisional Government?

3 Who were opposed to the Russian Revolution, and why?

1919: Treaty of Versailles

At the end of the First World War, the Treaty of Versailles made Germany give up land and pay a huge sum of money. Many Germans were very resentful about this. The Treaty also set up the League of Nations to safeguard world peace but, without American help, the League was not strong enough to stop aggressive nations.

1922: Mussolini seizes power in Italy

Mussolini and his fascist followers, known as 'blackshirts', marched on Rome and seized power in Italy. Mussolini became *Il Duce* ('the Leader') and set up an efficient but brutal rule over Italy. Soon Mussolini was demanding more land for Italy.

1927: Stalin seizes power in Russia

After a terrible civil war and famine, in which millions of Russians died, Stalin ('Man of Steel') took power in the Soviet Union. He immediately started putting his opponents to death, and began a ruthless programme to build up industry in the Soviet Union, killing anyone who stood in his way.

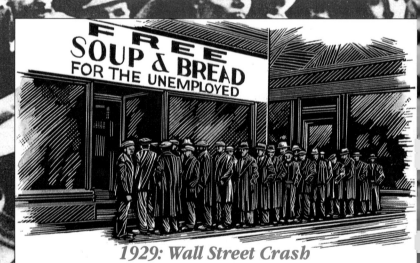

1929: Wall Street Crash

A great economic depression struck the world in 1929 and continued throughout the 1930s. There was mass unemployment with over 2 million in Great Britain, 6 million in Germany, and 15 million in the United States out of work.

OF AGGRESSION

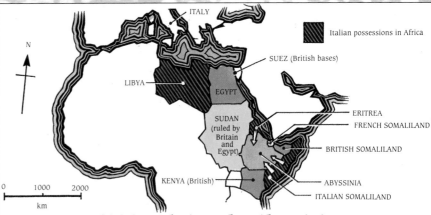

1935: Italy invades Abyssinia

Mussolini wanted to set up a new Roman Empire, so he began by attacking Abyssinia (modern Ethiopia). Using aircraft and poison gas, the Italians soon overcame the poorly-equipped Abyssinians. When the League of Nations protested at this aggression, Mussolini simply left the League.

1933: Hitler takes power in Germany

When Adolf Hitler promised Germans he would tear up the Treaty of Versailles, he won the elections and became Chancellor of Germany. He quickly gathered all power in his own hands and began arresting communists, trade unionists and Jews.

1938: Germany invades Austria and Czechoslovakia

Hitler met a warm welcome when he led his troops into Austria, but the Czech government seemed prepared to fight when he tried to take over the Sudetenland, an area of Czechoslovakia. However, when Britain and France told the Czechs to hand the areas over, the Czechs had to give in. The next year, Hitler took over the rest of Czechoslovakia.

1936: Spanish Civil War

In 1936, civil war broke out in Spain between the Republicans and General Franco's Nationalists. Mussolini and Hitler sent men and aircraft to help Franco. Stalin sent money to help the Republicans. After two years of bitter fighting, Franco won the war and took control in Spain.

7 Communist Russia

The Russian Revolution promised the Russian people, 'Peace! Bread! Land!', but it brought them 20 years of famine and terror.

Why did the Russian Revolution fail?

Stalin versus Trotsky

In 1924 Lenin died. Most Bolsheviks had assumed that Trotsky, Lenin's most trusted follower, would take over Russia. But Trotsky had enemies, especially the ambitious and ruthless Joseph Stalin. Over a number of years Stalin managed to get the upper hand. Eventually Stalin accused Trotsky of treason and sent him into exile. Stalin became the new ruler of Russia or the Soviet Union as it was now called.

The Five-Year Plans

Stalin's aim was to make the Soviet Union into a modern industrialised country as quickly as possible, so that it would not be at the mercy of rich capitalist countries.

Factories and mines were set high and completely unrealistic production targets in a series of Five-Year Plans which the workers had to meet. Anyone who protested or even questioned these quotas was shot or sent to a labour camp.

Many foreign visitors to the Soviet Union were impressed by what they saw. One American visitor, Lincoln Steffens, proclaimed excitedly, 'I have seen the future! And it works!' Lenin used to call visitors like these 'useful idiots'.

Source A

'Do you want our socialist fatherland to be beaten and to lose its independence? If you do not want this, you must put an end to its backwardness in the shortest possible time ... We are 50 to 100 years behind the advanced countries. We must make good this distance in ten years. Either we do it, or they crush us.'

Stalin, 1931

Source B

In this Soviet cartoon, a capitalist sniggers at the folly of the first Five-Year Plan until Russia's new factories and industrial production figures silence him.

34

Alexei Stakhanov became a national hero during the first Five-Year Plan, for cutting record amounts of coal on his shifts. Other workers were encouraged to follow his example. In fact, the whole story was made up, to make people work harder.

Source D

Stakhanov cutting coal.

Source C

Alexander Ardenko was an engine driver in the new industrial city of Magnitogorsk. He took tremendous pride in his work.

'I drove a railway tank engine. It was small and powerful and very beautiful. I was very proud of it. It was very useful to Magnitogorsk, carrying the molten iron in eight-ton hoppers, six or eight at a time. I blew the whistle as much as possible. I didn't have to, but I wanted to. I was building the heartland of the working class.'

Alexander Ardenko, speaking in 1990

In August 1933, Stalin officially opened what was claimed to be one of the greatest of the achievements of the first Five-Year Plan: the Belomor Ship Canal. In fact, it had been built by hand by thousands of slave labourers, arrested for criticising Stalin. More than 100,000 of them died during its construction.

Source E

Slave labourers at the Belomor Ship Canal.

Collectivisation

Stalin was suspicious of Russia's huge population of peasants, especially the more prosperous peasants or *kulaks*. In 1929 he announced that all farmland was to be taken away from the peasants, and redistributed into new, state-run farms called collectives. These would produce food efficiently for the new industrial cities. Anyone who opposed collectivisation was accused of being a kulak. The penalty for that was death.

Many peasants destroyed their own crops and livestock to stop Stalin's men getting their hands on them. Stalin sent armed groups into the countryside to seize food by force. Some 7 million Russian peasants starved to death from 1932 to 1933.

Grain production in Russia	
Millions of tonnes	
1913	76
1928	69
1930	83.5
1931	69.5
1932	70
1933	68
1934	68
1935	75
1940	75
1945	47

Source F

A poster praising the work of the collective farms. At the bottom, a wealthy peasant (a kulak) is being accused of hoarding grain by angry peasants.

Terror

More than 20 million people were shot on Stalin's orders during the 1930s. Many of the victims were Stalin's old comrades in the Bolshevik Party; others were ordinary Russians who had done nothing wrong. It made no difference. Stalin preferred to get them to confess to crimes: it made up for the lack of evidence. This period of terror was known as the Purges.

Source G

People queuing for food in the Ukraine during the famine of 1932.

---

1 Explain in your own words what the Five-Year Plans were. The Western estimates for industrial production were always lower than the official Soviet figures. Why do you think this was so?

2 How many examples can you find in this unit of cruelty towards the Russian people? Why do you think Stalin's government was so ruthless?

3 What good things did Stalin's government achieve for Russia?

8 The USA: boom and bust

America came out of the First World War rich and, in the 1920s, she became richer. But, in 1929, her economy collapsed and the economies of the rest of the world with it.

Why did the Depression start in the USA in 1929?

American money

One country had done well out of the war: the USA. While the USA was neutral, American firms were able to sell goods that European firms had stopped producing. By 1918, the USA was the only country which was not faced with huge wartime debts. The only way the Allies could pay their wartime debts, and the Germans make their reparation payments, was by borrowing money from America.

Source A

A poster showing New York as the gateway to America.

NEW YORK CENTRAL BUILDING

PARK AVENUE, NEW YORK

AT THE GATEWAY TO A CONTINENT

The Allies owe money to the USA.

Germany owes money to the Allies.

The USA loans money to Germany.

Germany pays reparation to the Allies.

The Allies pay debts to the USA.

The debt cycle.

The American dream

Americans had always dreamt that theirs was a land where anyone, no matter how poor, could get rich and rise to the very top. In the 1920s, it seemed as if, for millions of ordinary Americans, the dream was real. Cars, radios, vacuum cleaners, washing machines and innumerable domestic gadgets were rolling off the production lines of America's factories. If people did not have the money in ready cash they could buy on hire purchase, and pay in instalments.

But the dream did not last. During the boom years there were already signs that all was not well. Half-a-million farmers went bankrupt when the demand from Europe for American corn collapsed after the war. When alcohol was banned in America, violent gangsters ran illegal drinking halls, called speakeasies. In the South, a secret society called the Ku Klux Klan attacked and terrified black and Jewish people.

37

The business of America is business

In 1924, the USA had a new President, Calvin Coolidge. 'The business of America', he said, 'is business.' Americans took their cue from him and there seemed nothing the enterprising Americans could not do.

Jazz from Harlem and the energetic (and shocking!) Charleston swept through America.

LIFE WOULD BE BLISS,
DANCED THROUGH LIKE THIS!

Source B

In 1927, Charles Lindbergh was the first man to fly solo across the Atlantic. In 1932, Amelia Earhart became the first woman to do the same.

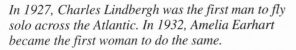

The little town of Hollywood, California, started producing spectacular films that captivated audiences the world over. This is the famous chariot race from one of the most popular, Ben Hur, which was made in 1925.

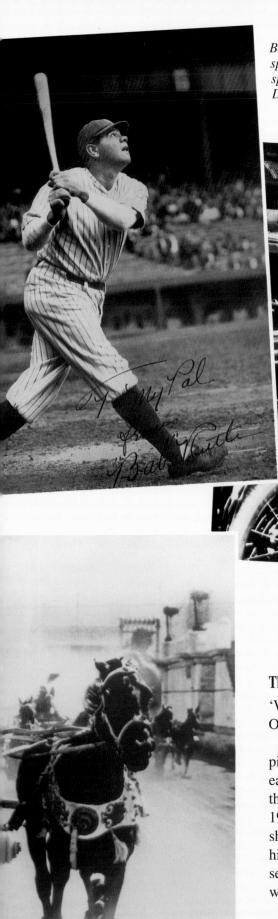

Baseball and boxing became mass spectator sports, producing some of the world's first sporting superstars, like the boxer Jack Dempsey and the baseball player 'Babe' Ruth.

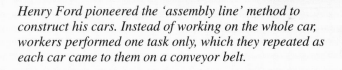

Henry Ford pioneered the 'assembly line' method to construct his cars. Instead of working on the whole car, workers performed one task only, which they repeated as each car came to them on a conveyor belt.

The Wall Street Crash

'WALL STREET LAYS AN EGG!', said the *New York Times* on 24 October 1929. The American stock market had collapsed.

Large companies are usually owned by shareholders. A share is a piece of paper that entitles the owner to some of the company's profits each year. Many people buy shares so that, if the company does well and the price of the shares increases, they can sell them at a profit. In the 1920s, thousands of ordinary Americans started buying and selling shares. The more people bought shares, the higher share prices went; the higher share prices rose, the richer everyone would be when it came to selling. No one stopped to wonder what would happen if everyone wanted to sell at the same time.

On 24 October 1929, a great panic swept through the New York Stock Exchange on Wall Street: suddenly everyone was selling their shares, and the price of shares collapsed. People who held on to their shares found they were worthless. It became known as the Wall Street Crash.

39

The Crash had a terrible impact on the American economy. Many factories and farms went bankrupt. American banks could no longer afford to lend money to European businesses, so many of these failed. This world-wide economic collapse was known as the Slump or the Depression.

Source C

A man who has lost all his money in the Wall Street Crash is forced to sell his car.

The Slump

- Wall Street shares collapse
- American firms and banks go bankrupt
- American trade declines and loans to Europe dry up
- European firms go bankrupt
- Europeans and Americans cannot afford to buy raw materials
- Third World producers of raw materials cannot sell their produce
- European governments try to raise money through high import duties
- World trade slumps
- Unemployment spreads world-wide
- Hunger marches take place
- Support for extremist political parties grows

Wall Street share prices

	US Steel	Radio Corporation of America	General Electric
	$	$	$
1928	138	94	128
1929			
3 Sept	279	505	296
24 Oct			
a.m.	205	68	315
p.m.	193	44	283
1930	182	48	75
1931	145	24	50
1932	48	9	21
1933	24	4	12

1 Look carefully at the summary of the Slump. Explain in your own words why what happened in America was so important to the rest of the world.

2 Explain in your own words what happened in the Wall Street Crash.

9 Britain and the USA: democracy between the wars

While some other countries became dictatorships in the 1920s and 1930s, democracy survived in Britain and the USA.

Why was there no revolution in the democratic states of Britain and the USA?

Britain: the General Strike

There was large-scale unemployment in Britain after the war. Even where men had jobs to go back to, they often found that factory owners wanted to make savings by cutting wages and making the men work longer hours.

In May 1926, the miners' leaders, Herbert Smith and A. J. Cook, called their men out on strike in protest. The Trade Union Congress (TUC) called all the other unions out on strike as well, to support the miners.

Railways, newspaper presses, factories, shipyards – the whole of Britain's industry stopped working. Volunteers rushed to keep essential services running. The Prime Minister, Stanley Baldwin, accused the strikers of trying to start a revolution, but the strikers said they were only trying to protect their wages. After nine days, the strikers could not afford to stop working any longer and had to go back to work.

Source A

The Labour MP, Ellen Wilkinson, took part in the most famous hunger march, the Jarrow Crusade, in 1936. The marchers walked from the north-eastern town of Jarrow to London to plead for help for unemployed shipyard workers.

The Slump and the hunger marches

The Wall Street Crash hit Britain very badly. Many shipyards and factories had to close. By 1930 there were 2.5 million people out of work in Britain.

There was real hunger in some areas where unemployment was high. Unemployed men staged hunger marches from these areas to London to get the government to help them. The Labour Prime Minister, Ramsay MacDonald, thought it was necessary to cut unemployment benefit. Some ministers resigned in protest, so, in 1931, MacDonald joined a coalition with the Conservatives to form a new National Government. The National Government made the cuts and borrowed £80 million from America. Slowly British trade began to recover and new jobs were created.

Extremist groups attracted some support during the Slump. Sir Oswald Mosley's British Union of Fascists and the British Communist Party broke up each other's meetings and marches, often very violently. The fascists also attacked Jewish people in the East End of London. The level of support for fascists and communists did not threaten the position of the democratic parties in Britain, as they did in Germany and Italy.

For many the standard of housing improved. Councils began to pull down some of the old slum housing and build new 'council houses' for people to rent.

Office workers and their families could afford a new semi-detached house with a garden, front and back, in one of the new suburbs.

People in work often went to the pictures two or three times a week, or listened at home to drama and dance music on the wireless.

Source B

Police clearing the streets of anti-fascist demonstrators after the British Union of Fascists' May Day march, through south-east London to Bermondsey, in 1938.

Suburban life in Britain

Not all of Britain suffered during the Slump: in some areas, especially in central and southern England, there were new industries producing electrical goods like radios or vacuum cleaners. William Morris built a huge car factory at Cowley in Oxford.

Why not live at Sudbury Hill?
Small, modern, labour-saving houses with garages and gardens.
Live in the country where you will have room to breathe.
40 minutes to Charing Cross. 50 minutes to Mansion House.

SEASONS Charing Cross · · 1 Month 24/6 3 Months 67/6
Mansion House · · 26/6 72/6

 UNDERGROUND

Source D

A poster issued by London Underground in the 1930s.

Source C

Refrigerators being manufactured at a factory in Luton, Bedfordshire, in 1932.

Ireland

At the beginning of the First World War, Ireland was ruled by Britain (as it had been for many centuries). At Easter 1916, armed Irish nationalists staged an uprising in Dublin to make Ireland independent. The rebellion was defeated and many of its leaders were shot. After 1918, the survivors of the Easter Rising called themselves the Irish Republican Army (IRA). They began a more widespread rising all over Ireland. In 1921, after three years of savage violence on both sides, the British Prime Minister, Lloyd George, agreed to meet the IRA leader, Michael Collins. They signed a treaty which allowed much of Ireland to become an independent state, but kept six of the counties in the northern province of Ulster as part of the United Kingdom. In these counties the majority of the population were Protestant Unionists who wanted no part in an independent Ireland.

The abdication crisis

In 1936 the monarchy was rocked by a major crisis. King George V died, and the Prince of Wales became King Edward VIII. But the new king wanted to marry an American, Mrs Wallis Simpson, who had already divorced one husband and was in the process of divorcing another. The Prime Minister, Stanley Baldwin, told the king that if he married Mrs Simpson, he could not continue as king. Edward VIII decided to abdicate (give up the throne), and his brother became King George VI.

Source E

The gutted remains of the General Post Office, Dublin, the headquarters of the Irish Nationalists during the Easter Rising of 1916. It was the scene of fierce fighting.

Source F

This song appeared in America in 1932:

'They used to tell me I was building a dream
With peace and glory ahead;
Why should I be standing in line
Just waiting for bread?
Once I built a railroad, made it run,
Made it race against time;
Once I built a railroad, now it's done –
Brother can you spare a dime?
Once w'khaki suits, gee we looked swell,
Full of that Yankee Doodle de dum
Half a million boots went slogging thro' hell,
I was the kid with the drum.
Say, don't you remember, they called me Al,
Gee, it was Al all the time;
Say, don't you remember
I'm your Pal! Buddy
Can you spare a dime?'

(Dime: an American 10 cent coin.)

E. Y. Harburg, *Brother, Can You Spare a Dime?*, 1932

America, after the Wall Street Crash, was a land of closed factories, long lines of unemployed men queuing for bread, and women trying to bring up children without enough money for food or clothes. President Herbert Hoover thought the best way to solve the crisis was to wait for American trade to recover in its own time. Most Americans were not prepared to wait that long. They nicknamed the shanty towns, that sprang up outside American cities, Hoovervilles, after the man they thought was to blame for what had happened to them.

There was a presidential election in 1932. Americans voted for the Democratic Party candidate, Franklin D. Roosevelt. Roosevelt promised action to get America back to work. He called it a 'New Deal for the American people'.

The 100 Days

Roosevelt set to work immediately. During his first 100 days in office, he reorganised the banks, cracked down on crime and fraud, and set up a whole series of government agencies to fight unemployment. They were nicknamed the Alphabet Agencies because they were known by their initials.

The Alphabet Agencies

- Civilian Conservation Corps (CCC) provided work on environmental projects.
- National Recovery Administration (NRA) made sure bosses treated workers fairly.
- Public Works Administration (PWA) ran big building projects, like bridges, highways and hospitals.
- Agricultural Adjustment Agency (AAA) advised farmers on how to make better use of their land.
- Tennessee Valley Authority (TVA) built hydro-electric dams and revived agriculture in the Tennessee valley.

Source G

Unemployed men in New York City lining up for the chance of a cheap meal.

Source H

An unemployed worker selling cheap apples outside his shanty home.

Source J

Mrs Eleanor Roosevelt supported her husband vigorously, often travelling round the country to speak to audiences about the New Deal:

'You may feel that there is nothing you can do in the face of this emergency. That isn't true. Thousands of women in this country have decided to do whatever they can, to find work for themselves and their husbands. Thousands are struggling to maintain their families in very difficult circumstances. They won't be told that they should give up, that the struggle isn't worthwhile. They won't believe it. And neither should you.'

Source K

Working people were very clear how they felt about Roosevelt's New Deal:

'A farmer: I would be without a roof over my head if it hadn't been for the government loan. God bless Mr Roosevelt and the Democratic Party, who saved thousands of poor people all over this country from starvation.

A worker: Mr Roosevelt is the only man we ever had in the White House who would understand that my boss is a son-of-a-bitch.'

Quoted in Hugh Brogan, *The Pelican History of the United States of America*, 1985

Source I

In his first speech as President, Roosevelt declared:

'Our greatest primary task is to put people to work. I shall ask Congress for broad executive power to wage war against the emergency, as great as the power that would be given me if we were in fact invaded by a foreign foe.'

Roosevelt, 1933

Fireside chats

Roosevelt was good at explaining his policies to ordinary people in a series of fireside chats over the radio. He used simple language to explain about complicated issues, like banking or economic recovery, so that everyone could understand what he was doing.

Source L
President Franklin D. Roosevelt.

Source M

This extract gives an idea of how Roosevelt's fireside chats sounded:

'The simplest way to judge recovery lies in the plain facts of your own individual situation. Are you better off than you were last year? Are your debts less burdensome? Is your bank account more secure? ... A few timid people, who fear progress, will try to give you new and strange names for what we are doing. Sometimes they call it "Fascism", sometimes "Communism" ... But in so doing, they are trying to make very complex and theoretical something that is really very simple and very practical ... All that we do seeks to fulfil the historic traditions of the American people.'

Roosevelt

The Dustbowl

In 1934, huge dust storms covered the western states of Kansas, Oklahoma, New Mexico, Texas and Colorado. After years of poor farming methods, the wind lifted the topsoil into the air and blew it for miles – some of it even fell on ships out in the Atlantic. The farmers in the area had to abandon their farms and set off to find work further west, in California. Roosevelt had to set up more special agencies to compensate the ruined farmers and help them get started again.

Source N

A dust storm hits a town in Colorado in 1937.

Hollywood films like *The Wizard of Oz* helped Americans to forget about the effects of the Depression.

Source P

A refugee from the sandstorms.

Source O

A scene from one of the most popular films of the 1930s – The Wizard of Oz.

1 What was the General Strike? Why did it fail?
How did the British government respond to:
a the economic crisis
b the crisis in Ireland
c the abdication crisis?

2 Explain in your own words what the New Deal was.

3 How did President and Mrs Roosevelt try to win popular support for New Deal policies?

4 What evidence is there in this unit that some people suffered between the wars while other people did well?

5 Using all the evidence in this unit, explain why Britain and the USA did not become dictatorships in the 1930s.

10 Fascist Italy

Under the leadership of Benito Mussolini, Italy became a fascist dictatorship.

How did Mussolini take control of Italy?

Italy: a 'Mutilated Victory'

Italy fought on the winning side in the First World War, but she was not given as much land in the peace settlement as she had hoped. The Italians felt cheated, and talked of the peace settlement as the 'Mutilated Victory'.

Italy's government was too weak and divided to do anything about this, or even to keep order at home. Prices and unemployment soared, and Italian workers went on strike. It looked as if Italy might have a revolution. In desperation, many Italians turned to a new political party, the Fascist Party, led by a journalist, Benito Mussolini.

Mussolini's march on Rome

Mussolini formed a fascist 'combat squad' of ex-soldiers, known as the Blackshirts. Soon they had a fearsome reputation for beating up socialists and trade unionists in the street, often while the police stood by.

By 1922, Mussolini felt strong enough to seize power. He said that he was the only one who could stop the violence on Italy's streets – which was not surprising, since most of it was the work of his own supporters. Mussolini was hoping to seize power by force but, rather to his surprise, the king and the government agreed to his demands. Following this, he and his supporters put on their uniforms, took the train to Rome and marched through the streets. The fascists called this the 'March on Rome'.

Source A

A poster showing Mussolini and some of the leading fascists of the 1920s.

Source B

At the end of their March on Rome, fascist Blackshirts gather outside the Royal Palace.

Mussolini's dictatorship

Mussolini changed the election law, so that the party which got a majority of the votes (however small) would receive two-thirds of the seats in parliament.

In 1924 his Blackshirts kidnapped and murdered Giacomo Matteotti, the leader of the Socialists in the Italian parliament and Mussolini's most fearless opponent. Mussolini spoke to the members of parliament about the murder. He said the murder was his fault because he had not been tougher on the street violence. He would need to take complete power. Parliament agreed.

Mussolini is always right!

Battle for grain	Battle for land	Battle for births
Big increase in wheat production	Pontine Marshes outside Rome are drained for building	Big rewards for mothers of large families, and taxes on bachelors
but	*but*	*but*
at the cost of other crops	other projects are not carried through	Italian birth rate continued to decline

Source C

Mussolini ended his speech to parliament after the murder of Matteotti with these words:

'I declare before all Italy that I assume full responsibility for what has happened ... Italians want peace and quiet, and to get on with their work. I shall give all of these, if possible in love, but if necessary by force.'

Il Duce

Mussolini was known as Il Duce, the leader. Fascist Party members paraded in smart new uniforms chanting their new slogan, 'Mussolini is always right!' Foreign visitors saw clean streets, efficient railways (at least on the popular tourist routes) and the world's first motorways. Many of them were very impressed.

Source D

After the Pontine Marshes were drained, four new cities were built on the reclaimed land. Here, Mussolini is cutting the first sod for the foundations of the new city of Aprilla.

Source E

The Italian novelist Primo Levi opposed Mussolini and later wrote a novel about life in fascist Italy.

'The local fascist schoolmaster spoke from the balcony of the town hall. He enlarged on the eternal grandeur of Rome, the seven hills, Caesar's legions and the Roman Empire about to be revived. He said the enemies of Rome would bite the dust and we would once more tread triumphantly on Roman roads, for Rome was everlasting ... Huddled against the wall below, the peasants listened in silence, shielding their eyes from the sun and looking, in their black suits, as dark and gloomy as bats.'

Primo Levi, *Christ Stopped at Eboli*, 1945

The 1929 election results

Percentage of electorate who turned out to vote	90%
Votes for fascists	8,500,000
Votes against fascists	135,000

The fascists were named after the 'fasces', a bundle of rods bound round an axe which were a symbol of authority in ancient Rome. The rods and axe represented the power to punish, and they were bound together to represent strength in unity. Mussolini borrowed many symbols from the Romans, including laurel wreaths, imperial arches, and their dreams of ruling a mighty empire.

The Fascist state

Il Duce

↓

Fascist Grand Council

Church	Schools	Workers
supports Mussolini in return for independence for the Vatican State	totally controlled by fascists, who decide what children should learn	Trade unions abolished and replaced by corporations representing workers and bosses

Source F

A poster showing Mussolini announcing Italy's entry into the Second World War in 1940.

1 Why were many Italians unhappy after the First World War?

2 How was Mussolini able to take power?

3 What did Mussolini do once he was in control of Italy?

4 What evidence is there in this unit that the Italian people genuinely supported Mussolini?

11 Germany: the Weimar Republic and the rise of Hitler

A fragile democracy was set up in Germany after the First World War. This was destroyed by Adolf Hitler and his Nazi Party followers.

What were the reasons for Hitler's rise to power?

The Weimar Republic

At the end of the First World War, the Germans over-threw the Kaiser and set up a republic. The new government met for the first time in the little town of Weimar, so it became known as the Weimar Republic.

The Weimar Republic had many enemies within Germany. The two groups who were most hostile, for quite different reasons, were the communists and the *Freikorps* (Freecorps).

- The communists were led by Rosa Luxemburg and Karl Liebknecht. They called themselves the *Spartakists*, in honour of Spartacus, the slave who led a revolt against the Romans. When they tried to seize power, however, the government used the army and the Freikorps against them. They were arrested and murdered along with many others.

- The Freikorps were armed groups of right-wing German ex-soldiers who were determined to destroy the communists. They planned to overturn the Weimar Republic and, in 1920, they captured Berlin. In the end, their revolt came to nothing because of a general strike of left-wing workers.

Source A
Rosa Luxemburg in 1912.

Source B
A group of Freikorps soldiers on the Potsdamer Platz, Berlin, in 1920.

Reparations

All Germans resented the Treaty of Versailles and in particular having to pay reparations to the Allies.

Source C

A school girl wrote this for homework in the 1920s:

'We pay and pay to France, and borrow and borrow from America. The Rhine and the Ruhr are saved, but you will pay until you drop. From 1918 to 1988, pay, pay, pay, pay, pay: father, son, grandson, great-grandson, great-great-grandson.'

Wiener library, London

Inflation

To help pay reparations, the German government simply started printing more money. This money quickly lost its value. Prices began to rise so Germany held up reparations payments to France. By 1923, Germany was experiencing one of the highest levels of inflation in history.

What did Germany have to pay?

1919 **Treaty of Versailles**
No cash limit set
No end-of-payment date set

1921 **Reparations sum set at £6,600,000,000**
No end-of-payment date set

1924 **Dawes Plan**
American financier Charles Dawes proposes Germany pays a fixed sum each year, plus interest
No end-of-payment date set

1929 **Young Plan**
American financier Owen Young cuts the reparations bill by 75%
Payments to continue annually until 1988

In 1923 France sent troops in to occupy the Ruhr, Germany's industrial heartland, and to confiscate German industrial products. In protest, German workers in the Ruhr went on strike and German industry ground to a halt. Since German industry was not producing anything, the German mark collapsed in value and prices soared.

Source D
A French armoured car at Essen in the Ruhr.

The falling value of the German mark in 1923	
January	$1 = 20,000 marks
June	$1 = 100,000 marks
August	$1 = 5,000,000 marks
September	$1 = 50,000,000 marks
November	$1 = 630,000,000,000 marks

Source E

In 1923, paper money was worth so little that children could play with kites made out of banknotes.

For those with debts to pay, the inflation was good news, but it was a disaster for anyone with savings. Tram fares or loaves of bread cost billions of marks. People stopped using money and resorted to bartering instead.

The new German Chancellor, Gustav Stresemann, called in all the useless money and burned it. In its place he issued a new currency, and to make sure it had some value he persuaded the workers in the Ruhr to call off their strike. The French went home and Germany went back to work.

The Beer Hall Putsch

Adolf Hitler was born in Austria in 1889. He had ambitions to be an artist, but he was not talented enough. In 1914, he joined the German army and won the Iron Cross, Germany's highest award for bravery. Like other soldiers, Hitler was aghast when Germany lost the war. He insisted that Germany had been 'stabbed in the back' by the men who had signed the armistice in November 1918. He called them the 'November Criminals'.

After the war, Hitler joined a small group called the German Workers Party. Hitler soon became its leader, and changed its name to National Socialist German Workers Party, or Nazi for short. With the inflation of 1923, Hitler thought the time was ripe for his party to seize control in Germany. With a group of ex-soldiers, including a wartime air ace, Hermann Göring, and Field Marshal Ludendorff, the Nazis plotted to seize control of Munich, the capital of Bavaria, and then stage a march on Berlin.

It was a shambles. The plotters had not planned things properly and Hitler lost his nerve. He spent most of the crisis making speeches to his own supporters in a beer hall. When Ludendorff finally persuaded him to lead a march through the streets, the police fired on the marchers and Hitler and the Nazis ran away. Two days later he was arrested.

Hitler received a five-year sentence for the Munich Putsch, but the prison was very comfortable and he was let out after a year. He spent the time writing a book about his ideas, *Mein Kampf* (My Struggle). In *Mein Kampf*, Hitler said that Jewish people were evil and sub-human, and that Germany should conquer a new empire in eastern Europe and Russia.

Source G

'Wherever I went [in Vienna] I began to see Jews, and the more I saw, the more sharply they became distinguished in my eyes from the rest of humanity ... Gradually I began to hate them.'

A. Hitler, *Mein Kampf*, 1924

Source F

Hitler and some of his supporters in Landsberg Prison.

Vote for Hitler!

After the failure of the Munich Putsch, Hitler decided to give up trying to seize power by force and sought election by legal means. His chance came after the Wall Street Crash in 1929. America stopped lending Germany money, and the German economy collapsed. Thousands of Germans were thrown out of work. In the election of 1932, the Nazi Party made a set of very attractive promises, based on what Hitler had written in *Mein Kampf*.

They promised to:

- tear up the Treaty of Versailles (including promises to pay reparations)

- build up the armed forces

- provide work for all

- reunite the Fatherland.

The Nazis also said the Jews were to blame for Germany's problems. Brown-shirted Nazi thugs, the *Sturmabteilung* (SA), beat up Jews in the streets.

The Nazis did well in the 1932 elections and, in January 1933, Hitler became the Chancellor (Prime Minister) of Germany.

Source H

An election poster produced for the 1932 German election. 'We farmers are mucking out. We vote National Socialist (Nazi Party).'

- *The other people shown on the poster represent communists and Jewish financiers. What do you think is meant by 'mucking out'?*

55

Source I

Hitler was made Chancellor, in January 1933, a short while after the elections.

Hitler seizes power

Shortly after Hitler gained power the *Reichstag* (parliament) building went up in flames. The Nazis said it was a communist plot to seize power. Hitler moved quickly.

- The Reichstag passed the Enabling Law, which allowed Hitler to rule without parliament.

- All political parties except the Nazi Party were banned.

- Trade unions were abolished, and Trade union leaders sent to concentration camps.

- Hitler ended reparation payments and pulled Germany out of the League of Nations, which she had joined in 1925.

Source J

Marinus Van der Lubbe, a young Dutch communist, here seen at his trial, was found guilty of starting the Reichstag fire.

The Night of the Long Knives

Now he was in power, Hitler was embarrassed by the behaviour of his old street thugs, the SA. Shortly after dawn on Saturday 30 June 1934, squads of Hitler's new bodyguard, the black-uniformed *Schutzstaffel* (SS), knocked up SA members, put them up against walls and machine-gunned them. There was no secret about it. It became known as the 'Night of the Long Knives'.

Source K

Hitler openly defended the Night of the Long Knives:

'If anyone reproaches me and asks me why I did not resort to the regular courts of justice, then all I can say is this: In this hour I was responsible for the fate of the German people, and thereby I became the supreme judge of the German people.'

Quoted in William Shirer, *The Rise and Fall of the Third Reich*, 1973

Germany prepares for war

Hitler had a very simple solution to Germany's problems: she should rebuild her army and air force as quickly as possible.

At first, rearmament was done in secret: air force squadrons pretended to be civilian flying clubs, and army units pretended to be keep-fit clubs. German motorways carried civilian traffic, but were designed for moving troops.

Soon Germany's armed forces came into the open. A unit of the air force, the Condor Legion, gained combat experience bombing towns in Spain during the Spanish Civil War from 1936 to 1939. The German army was soon much larger than the 100,000 men allowed by the Treaty of Versailles and, in defiance of the Versailles Treaty, it marched into the Rhineland in 1936. In 1938 German troops occupied Austria. No one did anything to stop them.

Source M

Ernst Röhm, the leader of the SA (in the centre of the picture), and Göring (on his left). Hitler is giving the Nazi salute. Röhm was murdered on the Night of the Long Knives, a year later.

Source L

A Nazi rally of the 1930s.

Appeasement

In the late 1930s Britain and France followed a policy of *appeasement*. This meant giving in to Germany's demands in order to prevent a war. The British, led by their Prime Minister Neville Chamberlain, thought that the Treaty of Versailles was unfair anyway, and they would not fight a war to enforce it; the French liked the treaty, but they would not do anything without the British. You can see the areas the Germans took over on the map.

The hardest test for appeasement was when Hitler demanded that part of Czechoslovakia called the Sudetenland. The Czechs were allied to France and seemed ready to fight. To stop this, Chamberlain, Mussolini and the French Prime Minister all travelled to meet Hitler at Munich in September 1938. There they all agreed to hand the Sudetenland over to Germany. Deserted by their allies, the Czechs had no choice but to give in.

Source N

Chamberlain on his return from Munich on 30 September 1938 telling the crowd that there would be 'Peace in our time'.

● *Explain what he meant by the phrase 'Peace in our time'.*

Source O

'You only have to look at the map to see that nothing that France or Britain could do could possibly save Czechoslovakia from being overrun by the Germans, if they wanted to do it.'

Neville Chamberlain's diary, 20 March 1938

Saarland: voted to rejoin Germany in 1935
Rhineland: German troops invaded in 1936
Austria: taken over by Germany (the *Anschluss*) in 1938
Sudetenland: occupied by Germany in 1938
Czechoslovakia: Germany invaded in 1939
Poland: invaded by Germany and Soviet Union in 1939
Danzig Corridor: claimed by Germany in 1939

This map of Europe shows the expansion of Germany before the outbreak of the war.

War

Things hotted up in 1939. In March, Hitler suddenly took over the rest of Czechoslovakia. In August he signed a non-aggression pact with, of all people, Stalin. This said that the Soviet Union and Nazi Germany would work together and would not go to war with each other. They also agreed to carve up Poland between them. Hitler then started demanding land around the port of Danzig from Poland.

Source P

A cartoonist's view of the pact between Hitler and Stalin showing the dictators marching together.
● *Why do you think each is shown with a hand on his gun?*

This time Britain and France stood firm. On 1 September 1939, Germany invaded Poland without warning. Two days later, Britain and France declared war on Germany.

---

1 How successful was Hitler during the 1920s?

2 Why were the Nazi election promises of 1932 attractive to many Germans?

3 What did Hitler do once in power?

4 What was 'appeasement'? Why do you think it failed to stop the war?

5 A historian, A. J. P. Taylor, suggested that the end of the First World War was the key cause of the Second World War. Using all the evidence from this unit, say if you agree with him.

12 Blitzkrieg

Instead of years of weary slogging in trenches, as in the First World War, Britain and France were beaten back quickly and it seemed the war would be all over in a matter of months.

Why were the Germans so successful in the early days of the war?

A new type of attack

Secret German war plans were code-named after colours. The plan to attack Poland was called *Plan White*. It was to be a new type of attack, and it became known as *Blitzkrieg* (lightning war).

In a Blitzkrieg speed was vital. The idea was to create panic and confusion as quickly as possible.

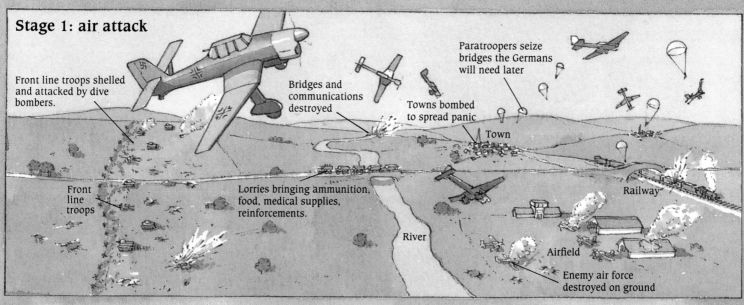

Stage 1: air attack

Front line troops shelled and attacked by dive bombers.

Front line troops

Bridges and communications destroyed

Lorries bringing ammunition, food, medical supplies, reinforcements.

Paratroopers seize bridges the Germans will need later

Towns bombed to spread panic

Town

River

Airfield

Enemy air force destroyed on ground

Railway

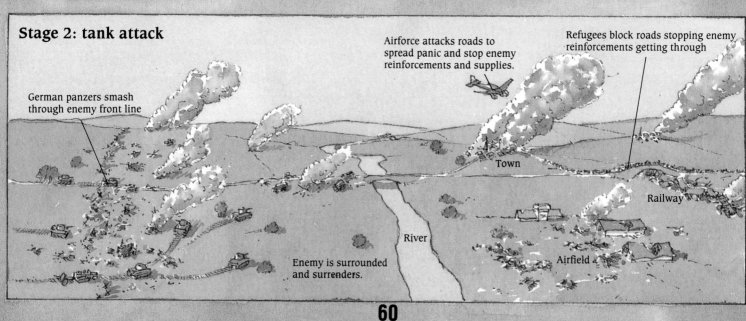

Stage 2: tank attack

German panzers smash through enemy front line

Airforce attacks roads to spread panic and stop enemy reinforcements and supplies.

Refugees block roads stopping enemy reinforcements getting through

Town

River

Enemy is surrounded and surrenders.

Railway

Airfield

How Blitzkrieg worked

Plan White was a devastating success. On 1 September 1939, without any warning, German tanks (*panzers*) tore the Polish army to pieces. The roads were so badly clogged with refugees that the Polish tanks could not get through, and the Poles had to send their cavalry in against the panzers. The horses stood no chance against the German tanks. Soon the Poles were forced back to their capital, Warsaw.

Source A

The JU87 Stuka dive bomber was specially equipped with sirens to make its bombing attacks even more terrifying by spreading panic among the refugees trying to escape the advancing tanks and troops.

There, they were able to put up a stronger fight, and German casualties were high in their attack on Warsaw. But on 17 September disaster struck for the Poles: the Russians invaded Poland from the east. Caught between two huge armies, the Poles were forced to surrender.

Source B

Panzers (tanks) were an essential part of the Blitzkrieg.

Source C

A Polish officer who saw the Blitzkrieg remembered the German attack as an old man.

'We were a good cavalry regiment, able to fight infantry or cavalry, not German tanks. So the horses were used as quick transport and we fought as infantry. One-third of the soldiers had to stay with the horses; only two-thirds actually fought.
Virtually total air superiority allowed the Germans to penetrate the country deep beyond the front line.'

Jozef Garlinski, 1989

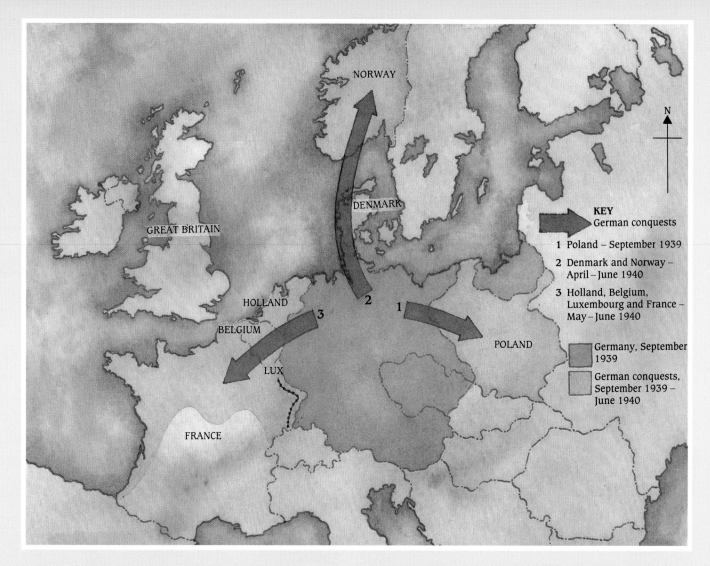

The beginning of the war in Europe. The first German conquests.

KEY
German conquests

1 Poland – September 1939
2 Denmark and Norway – April – June 1940
3 Holland, Belgium, Luxembourg and France – May – June 1940

Germany, September 1939

German conquests, September 1939 – June 1940

A Phoney War?

Meanwhile, in the west, nothing much seemed to be happening. The French sat behind a huge line of fortresses called the Maginot line. People nicknamed all the waiting around 'Sitzkrieg' or the Phoney War. When the Germans eventually attacked, they went around the Maginot line.

Hitler strikes to the north and west

On 9 April 1940, German troops tore through Denmark and landed in Norway. British and French troops managed to hold on to the port of Narvik for a time, and they sank ten German destroyers, but it was not enough: the Germans took control of Norway. In Britain, people were furious. Chamberlain was forced to resign, and on 10 May Winston Churchill became Prime Minister. But, that same day, disaster struck again. German troops smashed their way into Belgium and The Netherlands. Plan Yellow, the long-awaited German attack in the west, had begun. The Belgians surrendered quickly, but there was fierce resistance in The Netherlands before the Dutch surrendered.

Source D

Winston Churchill became the British Prime Minister after the fall of Norway.

Dunkirk

However, the main German attack was yet to come. It came through the forest of the Ardennes, where French defences were weak. German *panzers* raced across to the Channel coast and cut the Allied armies off from the rest of France. The Allies were forced back to the port of Dunkirk. And then the Germans did a very strange thing. They stopped.

The order to stop came from Hitler. We are still not sure why he gave it, but it gave the British time to launch *Operation Dynamo*: hundreds of ships and boats of all sizes, even pleasure craft, were sent across the Channel to rescue 300,000 British and French troops from the beaches at Dunkirk. The troops had to leave all their tanks and heavy guns behind, so although Operation Dynamo became known as 'the miracle of Dunkirk', really the Allies had been soundly beaten.

France defeated

On 14 June, German troops entered Paris and a week later France surrendered. The Germans forced the French to sign the surrender in the same place as the Germans had been made to surrender in 1918. France was to be divided in two. The northern half was to be occupied by Germany; the southern half was to be governed by Marshal Pétain, and became known as *Vichy France*. Pétain had been a French hero in the First World War, but now he had to learn to work with the Nazis.

Source F

Checkmate! Schach dem King! *A German propaganda cartoon from 1940 showing the King of England, George VI, in a corner of the chess board surrounded by a Stuka dive bomber, a paratrooper, a panzer tank and a U-boat. Chamberlain lies flat out while Churchill is fleeing.*

● *How did the cartoonist think the war was going for both sides?*

Source E

German victory parade in Paris.

1 Look carefully at the diagram on pages 60–61 and then explain in your own words how Blitzkrieg worked.

2 a What reasons can you find in Source C for the Germans' success in Poland?
b How many of these reasons are also shown in Source F? What other reasons does Source F give?

3 Why do you think the British called Dunkirk 'a miracle'? Were they right?

4 Why do you think that, by June 1940, many people thought Germany was going to win the war?

5 Using information from this unit, explain why the Germans were so successful in the early days of the war.

13 Britain embattled

'In six weeks, Britain will have her neck wrung like a chicken,' predicted a French leader in June 1940. At this time Britain was fighting virtually alone against a triumphant Germany. Britain seemed to face certain defeat.

How did Britain survive against the might of Germany?

The Battle of Britain

Hitler expected Britain to surrender after the fall of France, and he was surprised when Churchill refused to do so. Hastily, his generals drew up a plan to invade Britain. It was code-named *Operation Sealion*. It would mean crossing the Channel in the face of the powerful Royal Navy, so the Germans had to control the air above the Channel. Hermann Göring, the leader of the German air force, the *Luftwaffe*, promised to win control of the skies from the Royal Air Force. The defeat of the RAF would be the signal for an invasion of Britain.

1940 August

- German Luftwaffe attacks RAF airfields in southern England, but suffers heavy losses.
- RAF *Spitfires* and *Hurricanes* are guided to their targets by *radar* (radio detection and ranging), but suffer badly from attacks on their airfields and on radar stations.

1940 September

- Luftwaffe starts heavy bombing over London, which allows the RAF and radar stations to recover.
- Heavy Luftwaffe losses force Hitler to postpone Operation Sealion. Later he abandons it altogether.

The RAF pilots who fought in the Battle of Britain became known as 'The Few', after Winston Churchill honoured their victory with this speech:

'Never in the field of human conflict was so much owed by so many to so few.'

Source A

RAF pilots 'scramble' to their aircraft to intercept the approaching enemy aircraft.

British fighter planes attacking a German bomber formation. This modern illustration shows a Heinkel 111 bomber formation with Messerschmitt ME 109 fighter escort being attacked by Spitfires.

Source B

Women in operations room. When radar detected Luftwaffe bombers approaching, operations rooms like this directed the RAF fighter squadrons to intercept the enemy formations.

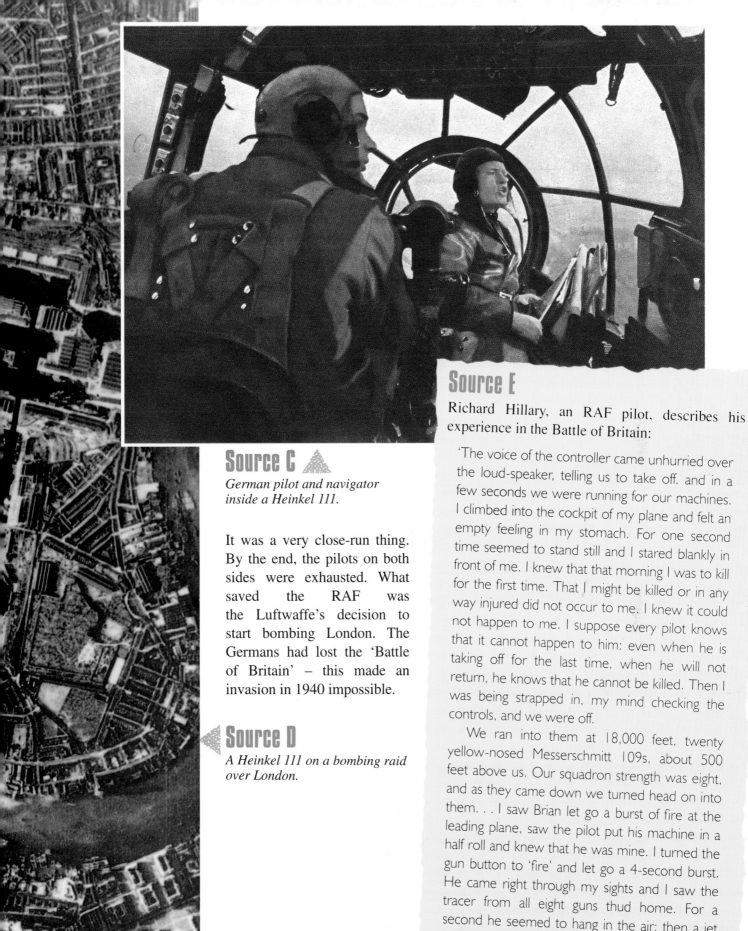

Source C

German pilot and navigator inside a Heinkel 111.

It was a very close-run thing. By the end, the pilots on both sides were exhausted. What saved the RAF was the Luftwaffe's decision to start bombing London. The Germans had lost the 'Battle of Britain' – this made an invasion in 1940 impossible.

Source D

A Heinkel 111 on a bombing raid over London.

Source E

Richard Hillary, an RAF pilot, describes his experience in the Battle of Britain:

'The voice of the controller came unhurried over the loud-speaker, telling us to take off, and in a few seconds we were running for our machines. I climbed into the cockpit of my plane and felt an empty feeling in my stomach. For one second time seemed to stand still and I stared blankly in front of me. I knew that that morning I was to kill for the first time. That I might be killed or in any way injured did not occur to me. I knew it could not happen to me. I suppose every pilot knows that it cannot happen to him: even when he is taking off for the last time, when he will not return, he knows that he cannot be killed. Then I was being strapped in, my mind checking the controls, and we were off.

We ran into them at 18,000 feet, twenty yellow-nosed Messerschmitt 109s, about 500 feet above us. Our squadron strength was eight, and as they came down we turned head on into them. . . I saw Brian let go a burst of fire at the leading plane, saw the pilot put his machine in a half roll and knew that he was mine. I turned the gun button to 'fire' and let go a 4-second burst. He came right through my sights and I saw the tracer from all eight guns thud home. For a second he seemed to hang in the air; then a jet of flame shot upwards and he spun out of sight...'

(Richard Hillary was later killed in action on 7 July 1943.)

The Battle of the Atlantic

Winston Churchill called the struggle to control the Atlantic the most important battle of the war. Britain depended heavily on importing food and oil from abroad, and it had to come by sea. The Germans sent submarines, called U-boats, to sink the ships. Hitler knew that he did not need to invade Britain. He could win the war by starving the British people into submission.

The ships stood a better chance when they sailed in groups called convoys, protected by naval escorts. The escort ships used Asdic, a sort of underwater radar, to find the U-boats, and depth charges to attack them. Even so, the U-boats were able to sink huge numbers of ships. It was not until 1943 that the tide began to turn: the Americans developed long-range aircraft that could hunt the U-boats far out in the Atlantic, and a new improved depth charge made it much easier for convoys to defend themselves.

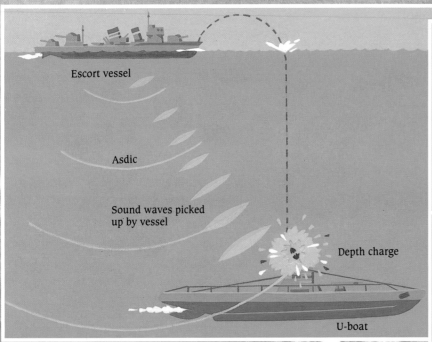

Asdic produces a sound echo revealing the enemy's position. Depth charges large explosive devices set to explode at the submarine's estimated depth, are then used to crush the pressure hull of the submarine.

Allied shipping losses in tons

Year	Tons
1941	4,100,000
1942	7,700,000
1943	2,900,000
1944	750,000
1945	250,000

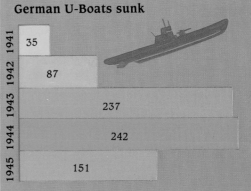

German U-Boats sunk

Year	Number
1941	35
1942	87
1943	237
1944	242
1945	151

Source F

A German U-boat shells a merchant ship, from a painting by H. R. Butler.

A FEW
CARELESS WORDS
MAY END IN THIS—

Source G

A propaganda poster showing the sinking of a merchant ship. Many posters in the Second World War had similar warnings about careless talk.
● Can you explain why?

Source H

Convoys could also be attacked by surface raiders like the German battleship Bismarck. In this painting by John Hamilton the Bismarck is being torpedoed by British aircraft during the Battle of the Atlantic in May 1941.

Soon afterwards it was sunk by Royal Navy ships. The Bismarck was unsuccessful as a surface raider – it had never attacked a convoy.

The Desert War

Towards the end of the Battle of Britain in 1940, Mussolini ordered his troops to attack British possessions in Africa. The British threw the Italians out and then invaded the Italians' own colonies, Abyssinia and Libya. 100,000 Italians, including six generals, surrendered.

The Germans were alarmed, and sent a large army, the *Afrika Korps*, under Field Marshal Rommel, to help the Italians. Rommel drove the British back, and in June 1942 he captured 25,000 Commonwealth troops at Tobruk.

Rommel felt encouraged to attack the British base in Egypt. The British commander, General Montgomery, was expecting the attack, and defeated Rommel in a massive battle at *El Alamein* in October 1942.

Source J

General Montgomery.

Source I

Field Marshal Rommel, known to his enemies as 'the Desert Fox'.

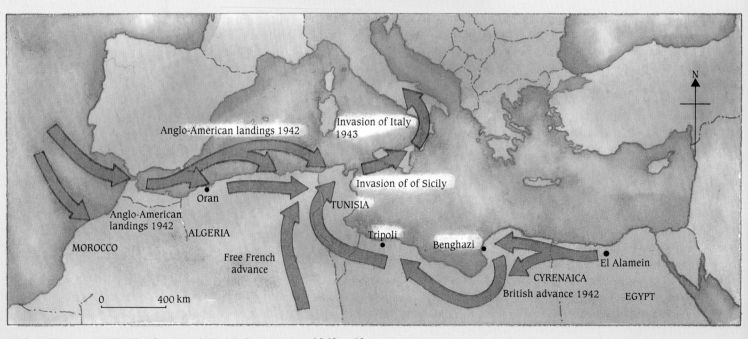

The war in North Africa and the Mediterranean, 1942 – 43.

Source K

Australian infantry attack at El Alamein.

Source L

A poster issued to show how all parts of the Empire gave support to Britain. Jewish, African, or West Indian troops who fought for Britain could expect little mercy from the Germans if they were captured.

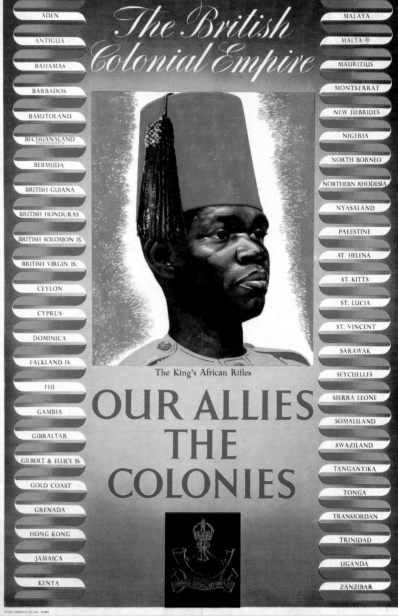

The British Colonial Empire

ADEN · ANTIGUA · BAHAMAS · BARBADOS · BASUTOLAND · BECHUANALAND PROTECTORATE · BERMUDA · BRITISH GUIANA · BRITISH HONDURAS · BRITISH SOLOMON IS. · BRITISH VIRGIN IS. · CEYLON · CYPRUS · DOMINICA · FALKLAND IS. · FIJI · GAMBIA · GIBRALTAR · GILBERT & ELLICE IS. · GOLD COAST · GRENADA · HONG KONG · JAMAICA · KENYA

MALAYA · MALTA · MAURITIUS · MONTSERRAT · NEW HEBRIDES · NIGERIA · NORTH BORNEO · NORTHERN RHODESIA · NYASALAND · PALESTINE · ST. HELENA · ST. KITTS · ST. LUCIA · ST. VINCENT · SARAWAK · SEYCHELLES · SIERRA LEONE · SOMALILAND · SWAZILAND · TANGANYIKA · TONGA · TRANSJORDAN · TRINIDAD · UGANDA · ZANZIBAR

The King's African Rifles

OUR ALLIES THE COLONIES

1 Look at this list of reasons why Germany lost the Battle of Britain. Explain in your own words how each reason made a difference to the outcome of the battle.
- The British had radar.
- The Germans started bombing London.
- The Germans miscalculated how many RAF planes they shot down.

Can you add any reasons of your own to explain why Germany lost the Battle of Britain?

2 a What was the Battle of the Atlantic?
b Why do you think Churchill considered it the most important battle of the war for Britain?

3 How successful was Britain in fighting the Desert War?

14 Home Fronts

On 14 November 1940 German bombers destroyed the centre of the medieval city of Coventry. Joseph Goebbels, the German Propaganda Minister, wrote in his diary that there was 'total helplessness in London'. In Germany, Hitler announced he wanted to build a new, strong German Reich (Empire) that would last a thousand years.

Was Goebbels right about Britain? What was life really like in Hitler's Germany?

Britain during the war

As more and more men went away to war, extra help was desperately needed in the factories and on the farms, so women were called up to work in industry, or to join the Women's Land Army and help feed the nation.

Source A
Women labouring in a steelworks.

Source C
Dig for Victory. People were encouraged to grow food on every available piece of land.

Source B

Wynne Bates joined the Women's Auxiliary Air Force (the WAAF) and trained as an electrician.

'We were met with absolute hostility. Until then, only men had been doing our jobs and they laughed at us women in big dungarees climbing up and seeing to the generators.'

Quoted in *The Independent*, 1991

Rationing

Food and clothes were in very short supply and had to be rationed, so it was important to be economical in cooking and shopping. Different goods, like vegetables and fruit, came on and off the ration according to how available supplies were. People with lots of money could buy more than their ration from black-market traders known as 'spivs'.

Invasion

In 1940 the Channel Islands fell to the Germans. If the RAF were to lose the Battle of Britain, there was a danger that the Germans would land in England. Volunteers joined the Home Guard to man road blocks and to practise blowing up tanks. The Home Guard was mostly made up of old men and, to start with, they had no uniforms or weapons, so it was just as well the Germans never actually landed!

Air raids

The biggest danger came from air raids. Whole areas of the City of London and the docklands were destroyed by German bombers in the Blitz. Other big cities like Birmingham, Liverpool, Bristol, Glasgow, Plymouth, Belfast, Newcastle and Manchester were heavily bombed too. Dover was shelled from Calais across the Channel. In 1942 the RAF bombed the historic German town of Lübeck, and in revenge the Luftwaffe bombed a number of historic towns like Exeter, York, Canterbury, Bath and Norwich, to try to damage British morale. To confuse the bombers, the government imposed a blackout. Windows had to be covered with heavy black material, and car headlamps were cut down to tiny slits of light. Factories often had large underground air raid shelters for their workers, or they used the basements of big hotels and department stores, and in London people also used the Underground. For the most part, heavy bombing merely made people more determined to win. But not surprisingly, people did sometimes get depressed and tired of spending each night in cramped shelters.

 Source E

A London bus in a crater. Photographs like this were often censored by the government.

Source D

People sleeping in the Underground to avoid the bombs.

Evacuation

There was no complete protection from air raids. When war broke out, children were evacuated from the big cities. Some went to Canada and America, until the ships carrying them began to be torpedoed. Most went to the country. For some children it was a great adventure, but many felt homesick and came home again.

Source G

A group of evacuees.

Growing up in Nazi Germany

The photograph in Source H shows a Nazi family in uniform. The girl is in the uniform of the League of German Maidens, and the two boys are members of the Hitler Youth. All children in Nazi Germany were supposed to join these organisations. Other youth groups, like the Scouts and Guides, were banned. Hitler Youth members swore loyalty to Hitler, the *Führer* (Leader), and paraded with drums and flags. At weekends there were hikes and camps in the countryside. It was all very good preparation for life in the army. At school, lessons and textbooks gave only the Nazi point of view. History lessons said how glorious Germany had been in the past and how unfair the Treaty of Versailles was. Everything bad was blamed on the Jews, and teachers encouraged pupils to hate the Jewish children in their class. The Nazis did not have everything their own way. Sometimes Hitler Youth patrols in the countryside were beaten up by gangs of rebellious teenagers called 'Edelweiss Pirates'. Even so, opposing the Nazis was very dangerous. It was only too easy to be arrested and sent to a concentration camp because of something you said or because of who your friends were. Even if you were released from the concentration camp, as some people were, memories of the beatings and the lack of food were enough to keep most people quiet.

Source H

A Nazi family photograph.

The treatment of women

All the powerful Nazis were men and they had a very narrow idea of how women should spend their lives. They talked about the three Ks: *Kinder*, *Kirche* and *Küche* (Children, Church and Kitchen); by this they meant that a woman's job was to be a mother, go to church and do the cooking.

Once they were in power, the Nazis began to stop women from doing better-paid work. Married women doctors and civil servants all lost their jobs. Women were not allowed to be judges. Courses in schools for girls were changed to put more emphasis on cooking and sewing and less on the qualifications needed for well-paid jobs.

Source I

Goebbels, the Nazi head of propaganda, did not think that women should go out to work.

'Woman has the job of being beautiful and bringing children into the world. Like a female bird she should preen herself for her mate and hatch her eggs for him.'

Joseph Goebbels, 1934

Source J

This poster from 1938 promotes the Nazi view of ideal youth and encourages young people to be involved with the Nazi cause.

Good times, bad times

Life in Nazi Germany could be pleasant. There were cheap holidays for working people arranged by the 'Strength through Joy' movement, and plenty of work making weapons or helping bring in the harvest. The war news was very good, at least to start with, and if you were in the forces there was the chance of a posting somewhere pleasant like Paris or Brussels. The German secret police, the *Gestapo*, controlled the occupied countries through terror. Newspapers and radio were censored, and no one was allowed out at night. Anyone caught listening to the BBC or writing anti-German graffiti would be sent to a concentration camp.

Collaborators

In many countries people were prepared to help or collaborate with the Germans, and, in all the occupied countries, plenty of people even volunteered to join the Schutzstaffel, or SS, which was a special Nazi army unit noted for its ruthlessness. The Norwegian Nazi leader was called Vidkun Quisling. 'Quisling' became a nickname for people in any country who helped the Germans.

Problems

Many Germans only really began to worry when the RAF began to bomb Berlin in August 1940. Hermann Göring had boasted that no enemy plane could ever drop bombs on Berlin, so the British raids came as a dreadful shock.

Source K

The Nazi Minister of Propaganda noted a change of mood in his diary.

'Morale slightly lower at home. Our people have to first accustom themselves to the thought of a second winter at war. I am receiving a whole series of complaining letters. We must conduct our propaganda more intensely and with more skill.'

Joseph Goebbels, October 1940

● What might the Germans have been complaining about?

The Germans were taken by surprise when they lost the Battle of Britain. It meant the war would not be over as quickly as they had hoped. The British were also blockading German ports so that food supplies could not get in. Soon the Germans had to start rationing food and clothing. They even had to ration bread, which was never rationed in Britain during the war.

Life under German occupation

What about people in the countries that were taken over by the Germans? What was life like for them? In some ways, life went on as normal. People still had to go to work, to school or to the shops, and all of these meant having to work with the Germans, because only they could issue identity cards, ration books and work permits. The Germans needed people to work in

Source L *Joseph Goebbels.*

their factories so they forced people in occupied countries to travel to Germany to work. In the Channel Islands, the Germans shipped everyone who had been born in Britain to Germany as forced labour. Forced labour workers were treated virtually as slaves, forced to work until they died from exhaustion.

76

ILS DONNENT LEUR SANG

DONNEZ VOTRE TRAVAIL
pour sauver l'Europe du Bolchevisme

Source M

A French poster calling for volunteers to work in Germany. As the war progressed people were forced to go and work in Germany.

● Why do you think there was a change from volunteer to forced labour?

1 Suppose you were a German spy in Britain. Using all the evidence from pages 72–74, write a report about what it was like in Britain. (You might need to twist some of the evidence!)

2 Some historians feel that British people were united in this period, while others feel that it was a period of disunity. How can historians come to such different conclusions?

3 What information in this unit suggests that
a some people enjoyed aspects of life in Hitler's Germany
b some people were badly treated in Hitler's Germany?

4 How can you explain the fact that people ruled by Hitler had very different opinions about him?

5 In what ways did life become harder for German people as the war went on?

Resistance

During the war, some people in occupied countries were prepared to fight against the Germans. The Germans were good at recruiting spies to get inside resistance groups and report back to the Gestapo. If the Germans could not catch resistance fighters, they took reprisals against innocent people. In 1942 Czech resistance fighters killed Reinhard Heydrich, the brutal head of the German secret police in Czechoslovakia. In revenge, the Germans picked at random a village called Lidice, and killed everyone in it. Then they burnt all the buildings and removed the village's name from maps and signposts.

The Soviet Union was a mighty power, with the largest army in the world, yet when the Germans attacked in 1941 they took the Russians by surprise and nearly reached the gates of Moscow.

Why was the Soviet Union so badly prepared for the war?

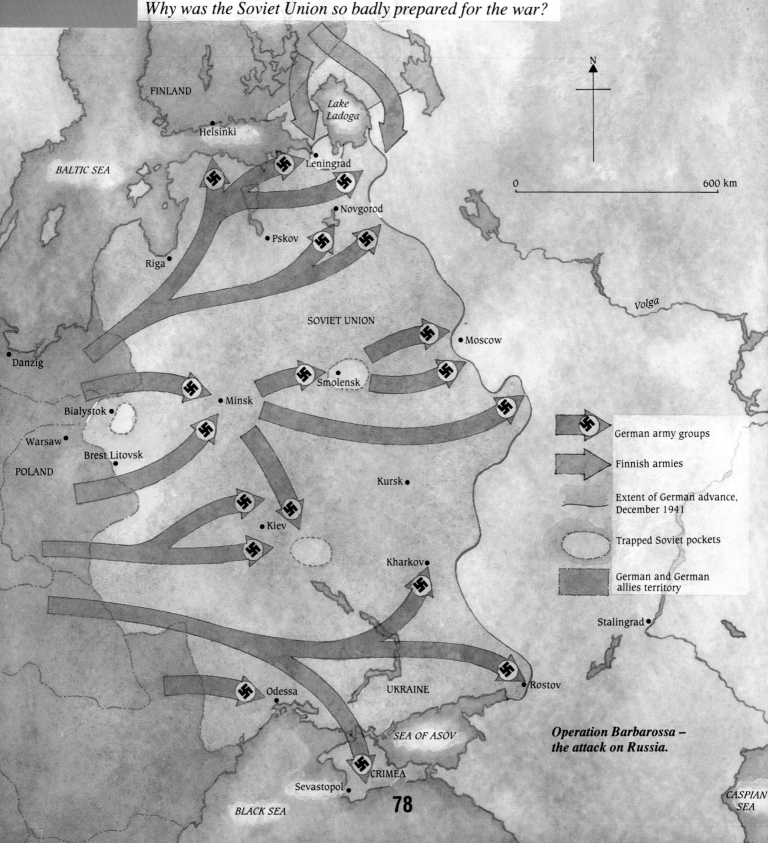

N

0   600 km

FINLAND

Lake Ladoga

Helsinki

BALTIC SEA

Leningrad

Novgorod

Pskov

Riga

SOVIET UNION

Volga

Danzig

Moscow

Smolensk

Bialystok

Minsk

Warsaw

Brest Litovsk

POLAND

Kursk

Kiev

Kharkov

Stalingrad

German army groups

Finnish armies

Extent of German advance, December 1941

Trapped Soviet pockets

German and German allies territory

Odessa

UKRAINE

Rostov

SEA OF ASOV

Operation Barbarossa – the attack on Russia.

CRIMEA

Sevastopol

BLACK SEA

CASPIAN SEA

The purges

After Stalin took power in the Soviet Union in 1927, he was terrified that his enemies would try to kill him. In 1934 a communist leader called Kirov was assassinated in Leningrad (actually on Stalin's orders, though no one knew this then). Stalin took the opportunity to have even more people arrested. They were put on trial and made to confess to huge crimes that they could not possibly have committed. Then they were sent to the *gulags* (concentration camps). These arrests were called *purges*.

Still Stalin did not feel safe. In 1937 he turned on the army. Thousands of officers were arrested and shot. Even the highest ranks were not safe. By 1939, the Red Army had lost half its officers, including three of its top five generals.

Most of the news about the purges was kept secret – as far as you can keep secret the arrest of millions of people, and the use of them as slave labour. But some people outside the Soviet Union knew very well what was going on. The Germans were particularly interested.

The Winter War

In December 1939 Stalin attacked Finland. It was the first proper war the Russians had fought since the purges, and they made a complete mess of it. The Finns beat them back easily, and it took months of fighting before the Russians forced the Finns to give in.

- Why do you think the Germans watched the events of the Winter War closely?

Hitler and the Soviet Union

Hitler hated the Russians.

- He thought Russians were 'sub-human'.
- There was a huge Jewish population in the Soviet Union, and Hitler hated Russian Jews even more than he hated other Russians.
- Hitler hated communism, and the Soviet Union was the only communist country in the world.
- The Soviet Union had vast areas of good farming land. This was the land Hitler wanted for the German people's *Lebensraum* (living space).

Die Gefahr des Bolschewismus

Source A
A German anti-Bolshevik poster.

Hitler made no secret of his feelings. The only real puzzle is why Stalin did not realise how Hitler felt.

Source B
Hitler set out his views on the Soviet Union many years before the war.

'When we speak of new land (for Germany) in Europe today we must principally bear in mind Russia and the border states subject to her.'

Adolf Hitler, *Mein Kampf*, 1924

Operation Barbarossa: 22 June 1941

The German attack was planned for June 1941. It was code-named *Barbarossa* ('Redbeard') after a German medieval hero.

The Russians were taken completely by surprise. The Germans destroyed the Russian air force on the ground, and smashed through the Russian defences. Surrounded and confused, over 600,000 Russian troops surrendered in the first week.

The Russians destroyed crops, bridges and railway lines in the Germans' path to stop them using them. They even managed to move over 1,000 factories and workshops out of danger and set them up hundreds of miles to the east. Even so, by November 1941 the Germans were just outside Moscow. On the Russian Front neither side showed the other any mercy, and it became a struggle to the death. It seemed that nothing could save the Soviet Union from total defeat.

Source C

Russian peasants try to save belongings as their village burns.

Source D

German troops in Rostov, 1941.

Clearing the land

The Nazis planned to clear the land they took in the Soviet Union to make room for German settlers, and that meant getting rid of the Russians who lived there. As the Germans tore into the Soviet Union, special army units called *Einsatzgruppen* followed them and began destroying whole villages and either murdering the people or sending them to slave labour camps.

Source E

A public hanging in occupied Russia. The Germans did not hesitate to execute anyone who opposed them in the Soviet Union.

Source F

Himmler, the head of the SS, gives instructions to his generals.

'Whether 10,000 Russian females fall down from exhaustion while digging an anti-tank ditch or not interests me only in so far as the anti-tank ditch for Germany is finished.'

1941

Some people, ruled by Stalin, welcomed the Germans. Non-Russians, like Latvians, Lithuanians, Ukrainians and Cossacks, decided that helping the Germans was the best way to win their independence.

Russian guerrilla fighters called *partisans* fought back against the Germans by burning crops, attacking German patrols or blowing up bridges or ammunition dumps. Like the Germans, they had no mercy on their enemies, and they expected none if they were caught.

Source G

Two young Ukrainian women partisans.

81

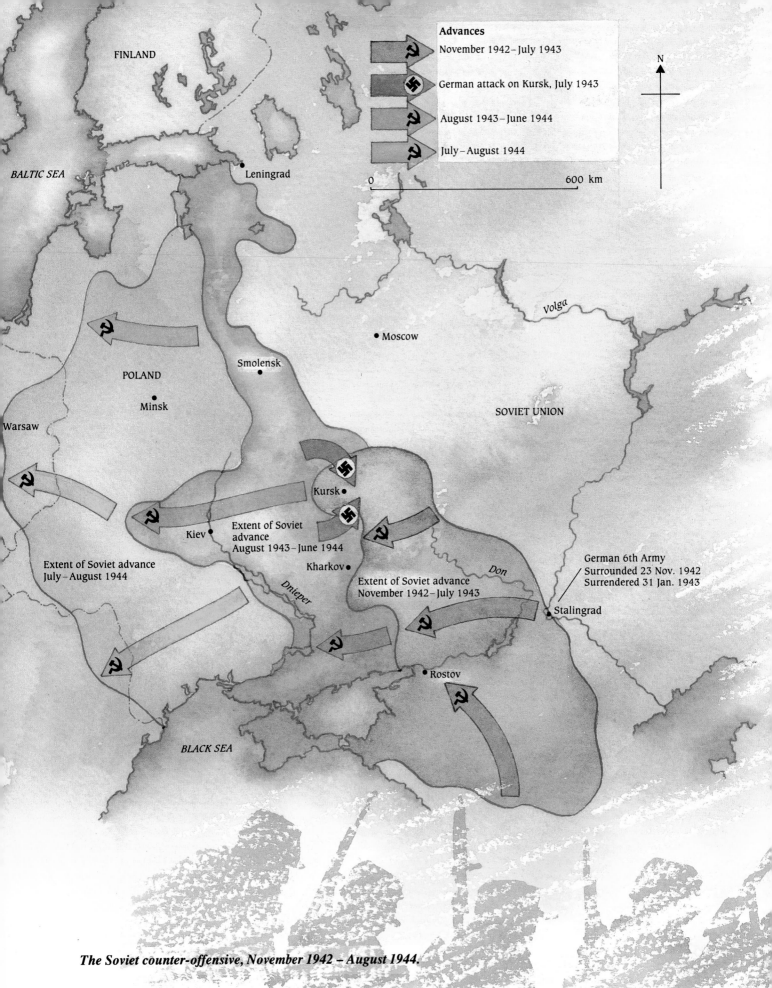

Advances

November 1942 – July 1943

German attack on Kursk, July 1943

August 1943 – June 1944

July – August 1944

0   600 km

N

FINLAND

BALTIC SEA

Leningrad

Moscow

Volga

POLAND

Smolensk

Minsk

Warsaw

SOVIET UNION

Kursk

Extent of Soviet advance
August 1943 – June 1944

Kiev

Extent of Soviet advance
July – August 1944

Kharkov

Dnieper

Don

Extent of Soviet advance
November 1942 – July 1943

German 6th Army
Surrounded 23 Nov. 1942
Surrendered 31 Jan. 1943

Stalingrad

Rostov

BLACK SEA

The Soviet counter-offensive, November 1942 – August 1944.

82

The Russians strike back

In December 1941 the Germans were just outside Moscow. The Muscovites dug anti-tank ditches and put up barricades. Stalin had his bags packed, ready to flee the city. Then he got some welcome news from Richard Sorge, his secret agent in Tokyo. Stalin was holding some of his best troops back in reserve in case the Japanese attacked the Soviet Union in the east. The message from Tokyo said that the Japanese were planning to attack the United States, not the Soviet Union. Stalin stayed in Moscow, and launched his reserves against the Germans. The Germans did not know what had hit them. They were forced back. As winter set in, their vehicles got stuck in deep mud and their weapons froze up and could not be fired. Moscow was saved.

But in the north, it was the Russians who were freezing. The Germans held the city of Leningrad, now known by its old name St Petersburg, in the grip of the worst siege in history.

The siege of Leningrad

The Germans cut Leningrad off from the rest of Russia and rained shells on it. Leningrad's beautiful palaces and churches were flattened. During the terrible winter of 1941, over 3,000 people starved to death every day. There were so many dead that they had to be buried in mass graves. Those left alive took to catching rats or crows to eat; then they began eating anything they could find, even Vaseline, sawdust, wallpaper paste and carpenter's glue. The siege of Leningrad lasted 900 days and nearly one million Leningraders died in that time.

Source H

Hitler's orders for Leningrad in 1941 were very clear:

'The Führer has decided to have Leningrad wiped off the face of the earth. The further existence of this large city is of no interest once Soviet Russia is overthrown ...'

Stalingrad

When the weather got better in 1942, the Germans hit back. They had a new plan to seize Russia's oil fields. The Germans caught the Russians by surprise and advanced very rapidly. Then the German commander, General von Paulus, decided to capture the city of Stalingrad. The Russians in Stalingrad fought fiercely for every building and every street. The whole city was reduced to rubble, but still the Russians would not give in. Von Paulus wanted to pull his men out but Hitler absolutely refused to allow it. Russian reinforcements arrived, and surrounded the Germans just as the terrible Russian winter was setting in. The Germans still did not have proper winter clothing, and they were running out of food and ammunition. They carried on fighting until January 1943, when von Paulus agreed to surrender. The Russians took nearly 90,000 Germans prisoner. This was a great turning point in the war. After Stalingrad the tide began to turn against Hitler.

Source I

Hitler's last message to von Paulus, in January 1943, reads as follows:

'Capitulation (surrender) is impossible. The 6th Army will do its historic duty at Stalingrad until the last man, in order to make possible the reconstruction of the Eastern Front.'

1 Why was the Soviet Union's Red Army so weak by 1941?

2 After the war, some people said that Hitler was not really to blame for the terrible things the Germans did. What evidence is there that Hitler was personally responsible for
● the terrible conditions in Leningrad
● the disaster at Stalingrad?

3 Why do you think the Germans failed to conquer the whole of the Soviet Union? Explain your answer.

4 Explain why the fighting in Russia was so bitter and vicious.

1941: Japanese attack Pearl Harbor

Without any warning, on 7 December Japanese planes bombed the American fleet at Pearl Harbor in Hawaii, and attacked British positions in Malaya. The Allies were taken completely by surprise, and the American fleet was badly damaged in the attack on Pearl Harbor.

1941: Japanese aircraft sink HMS *Prince of Wales and* Repulse

The British sent HMS *Prince of Wales* and HMS *Repulse* as a 'vague menace' to warn the Japanese not to attack the British base at Singapore. Without air cover the ships were defenceless when Japanese torpedo bombers found them and they were quickly sunk, taking hundreds of men to their deaths.

1942: Singapore surrenders to the Japanese

The Japanese swept through the British colonies in Asia, taking Hong Kong and Malaya. In February 1942 they took the mighty British fortress of Singapore. Singapore's heavy guns faced out to sea, but the Japanese attacked from the land. When the city's water supply ran out, the British commander had to surrender.

1942: Philippines fall to Japanese

General Douglas MacArthur led a fierce American defence of the Philippines, but the Japanese trapped the Americans in the narrow Bataan peninsula and forced them to surrender. As MacArthur left, he vowed 'I shall return'. As many as 10,000 Americans died in a terrible 'death march' from Bataan to prison camps in the north of the islands.

THE EAST

1942: Battle of Midway

The Japanese were steaming towards Midway Island in the middle of the Pacific when the Americans intercepted them. The battle was fought almost entirely by aircraft from aircraft carriers – the two fleets never saw each other. The Americans sank five Japanese carriers and lost one of their own. The Japanese were forced back in confusion.

1943: Americans retake Guadalcanal

After Midway, the Americans began the long, slow process of attacking Japanese-held islands in the Pacific. It was known as 'island hopping'. They began with Guadalcanal in the Solomon Islands, where the Japanese kept up fanatical resistance for six months before finally giving in.

1943–44: British fight back in Burma

Specially trained British groups called Chindits fought behind Japanese lines in the jungles of Burma. In 1944 the Japanese tried to invade India with a contingent of anti-British Indian troops, but they were thrown back after a battle at Imphal. In China the American General 'Vinegar Joe' Stilwell helped the Chinese guerrillas operating against the Japanese. Very slowly, the Japanese were pushed back through the jungle.

1942–45: Americans bomb Japan

In 1942 General James Doolittle led a surprise bombing attack on Tokyo. The Americans continued heavy bombing of Japanese cities, killing thousands in terrible firestorms. Finally, in 1945 they dropped atom bombs on Hiroshima and Nagasaki, devastating both cities.

16 Pearl Harbor

On 7 December 1941, Japanese planes attacked the American Pacific Fleet at Pearl Harbor. This brought the USA into the war.

Why did Japan decide to go to war with the strongest country in the world?

Understanding Japan

Japan in the 1930s seemed at first sight like any other modern country; but much of the country's old way of life survived. The Japanese still regarded their Emperor as a god. Many young Japanese officers were ready to fight and even die for their Emperor, like the samurai warriors of old. All they needed was a war.

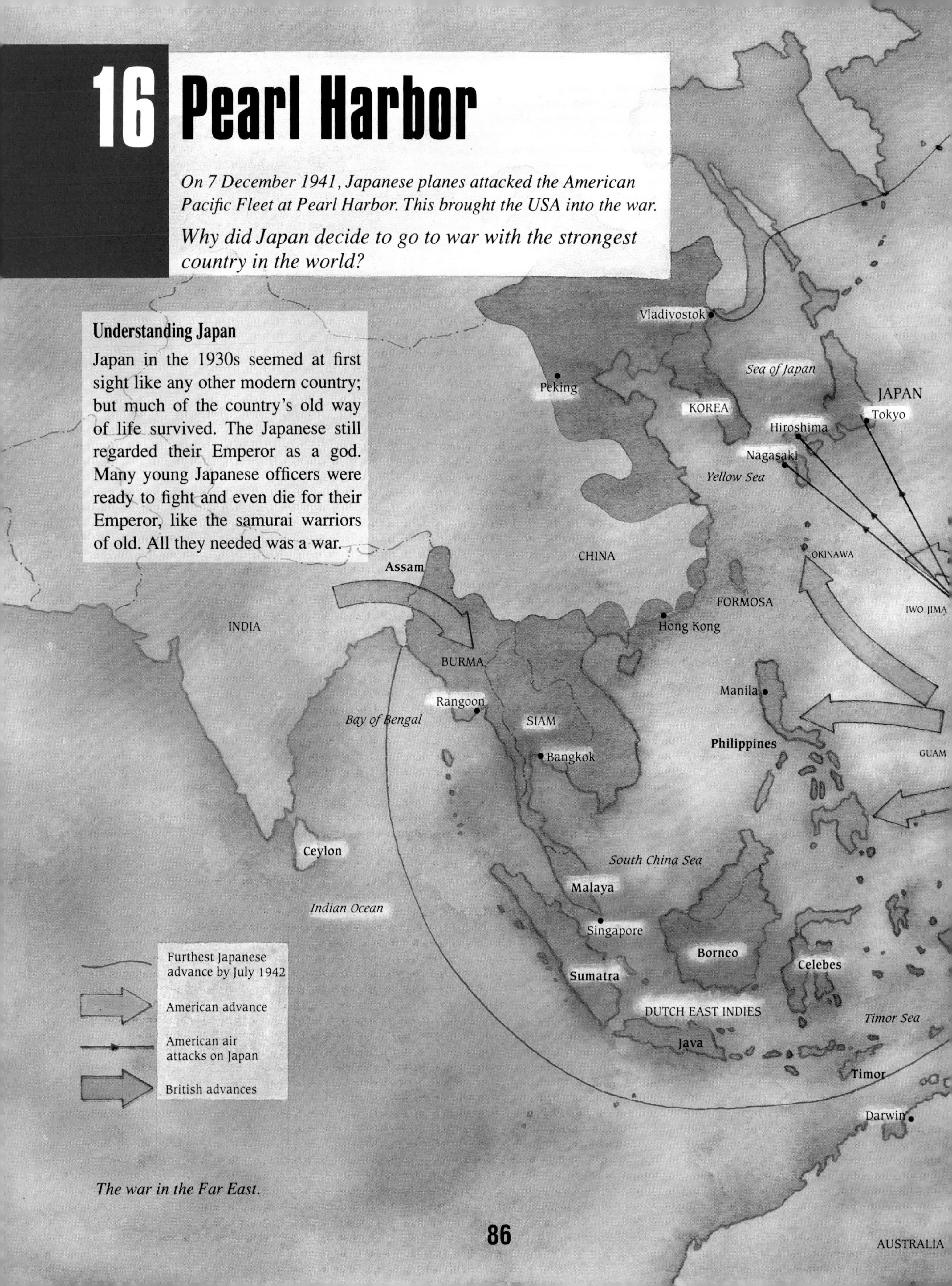

Vladivostok

Sea of Japan

Peking

KOREA

JAPAN
Tokyo

Hiroshima

Nagasaki

Yellow Sea

CHINA

OKINAWA

Assam

FORMOSA

IWO JIMA

INDIA

Hong Kong

BURMA

Manila

Rangoon

Bay of Bengal

SIAM

Philippines

GUAM

Bangkok

Ceylon

South China Sea

Indian Ocean

Malaya

Singapore

Borneo

Celebes

Sumatra

DUTCH EAST INDIES

Timor Sea

Java

Timor

Darwin

Furthest Japanese advance by July 1942

American advance

American air attacks on Japan

British advances

The war in the Far East.

AUSTRALIA

Japan had many problems.

- **Raw materials** Japan depended almost entirely on other countries for the raw materials needed for its industries.
- **Population** The country of Japan is a small group of islands, but the population was growing at an alarming rate. Vast numbers of Japanese people went to live in America. In 1924 the Americans began to limit the numbers of Japanese allowed in.

The 'solution'

In the late 1920s Japan's army leaders saw one simple solution to these problems: Japan should set up its own empire, just as the Europeans had done. This would bring in raw materials and provide somewhere for the country's huge population to live.

The army and the navy began to take control of the government. Politicians who protested were murdered. By 1931, Japan's leaders felt ready to begin their conquests.

The Japanese plan to build up an empire began in China. The Chinese were already fighting a bitter civil war, but they settled their differences for the moment in order to fight the Japanese. The Japanese found themselves bogged down in a long guerrilla war. Then, in 1941, the Americans cut off their exports of oil to Japan. Without oil, the Japanese could not keep their troops in China.

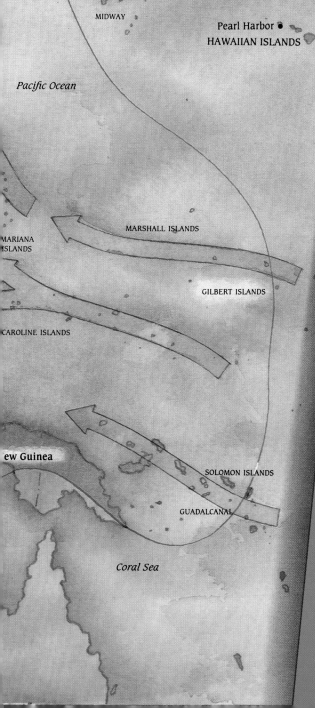

IMPERIAL JAPANESE GOVERNMENT

TOP SECRET

SUBJECT: Oil crisis

BACKGROUND

1. There is no sign of an end to the war in China. Our troops control all the important towns, but cannot control the countryside.

2. The Europeans and Americans demand that we should pull out of China. The Americans have now cut off oil exports. Without oil, our armies will have to pull out of China, and Japan will look weak and foolish.

THE PROBLEM

3. We must get hold of oil. There is plenty of oil in South East Asia. These areas, however, belong to the French, British and Dutch.

4. The French, British and Dutch are very weak. France and The Netherlands have been conquered by the Germans; the British are far too busy fighting the Germans in North Africa and Europe to defend their bases at Singapore and Hong Kong successfully. However, the United States is not at war, and will try to stop any move made by Japan to expand.

ACTION TO TAKE

5. We must have oil. Therefore we must conquer the British, Dutch and French possessions in South East Asia. They will not be able to fight back. We must find a way of crippling the Americans early on, before they have a chance to prepare. This means we must make a surprise attack.

The plan

Admiral Yamamoto came up with a plan to cripple the Americans. He discovered that on Sunday 7 December 1941 the whole American Pacific Fleet would be at anchor at Pearl Harbor in Hawaii. If the Japanese could destroy it, the Americans would be powerless to stop them taking over the Pacific and getting all the oil they wanted.

The attack

On the morning of 7 December, Japanese planes began bombing Pearl Harbor. The Americans were stunned. There had been no warning, and they could do nothing to fight back. Five battleships and four-teen other vessels were sunk. The American aircraft were all neatly grouped together, and were easily destroyed by the Japanese bombs. The Japanese flew back to their aircraft carriers in triumph. But was it a triumph? The ships sank in shallow water, and three of the battleships were repaired and set sail later in the war. Above all, the American aircraft carriers were not at Pearl Harbor on 7 December. Japan had started war with the United States, and would have to face the consequences.

Source B

Soon after the attack on Pearl Harbor, Admiral Yamamoto said:

'I fear we have only awakened a sleeping giant, and his reaction will be terrible.'

December 1941

Source C

Much later, historian A. J. P. Taylor wrote in 1961:

'The Japanese … never imagined they could penetrate to the New World and invade the United States. They did not even imagine that, if there were a prolonged war between them and the United States, they would win it. What they hoped for was that the United States, mainly involved in the European war, with so much of its resources directed towards Europe, would weary and would, in the end, come to a compromise with Japan.'

Source A

Pearl Harbor, 8.40 a.m., 7 December 1941. The American fleet is destroyed by Japanese aircraft.

1 Explain in your own words why the Japanese decided to build up an empire.

2 Put yourself in the position of the Japanese leader Admiral Yamamoto, just before Pearl Harbor. Write a top-secret letter to Emperor Hirohito explaining why you have decided to launch a surprise attack on the USA.

17 The Holocaust

Of all the many atrocities in the Second World War, none was more horrifying than the Holocaust: the Nazis' attempt to exterminate the entire Jewish race.

Why did the Nazis commit this appalling crime?

Anti-Semitism, as hatred of Jewish people is called, had been common in Europe for many centuries. There had been massacres of Jewish communities in several European countries since the Middle Ages.

The Nazis were violently racist. From his earliest days, Hitler loathed Jewish people. He even thought that the defeat of Germany in the First World War and the communist revolution in Russia were part of a Jewish plot to take over the world.

Source A

In one of his earliest speeches Hitler blamed the Jews for the problems of the world.

'Already the Jews have destroyed Russia and now they turn on Germany. Out of envy the Jews want to destroy the spirit of Germany.'

Hitler, July 1922

Source B

A Jewish store daubed with Nazi graffiti, Berlin, 1933.

Once in power the Nazis turned on the Jews of Germany. In 1933 Jews were banned from doing a number of well-paid jobs. Jews could not be German citizens and Jews were not allowed to marry other Germans. Nazi stormtroopers beat up Jews in the street, and a special newspaper printed anti-Jewish propaganda. Although they were the victims of violence and abuse, the destruction of the Jews was not an overnight event. In November 1938 there was a sign of even worse things to come when, in one night, synagogues were burned down all over Germany and many hundreds of Jews were murdered. Thousands of Jewish shops and homes were attacked; there was so much broken glass that the night became known as 'Kristallnacht' – the Night of Broken Glass. The Nazis even made their Jewish victims clear up the glass.

Source C

Paris, 1940, a Jewish man wearing a yellow star. In Germany and all occupied countries the Nazis forced Jewish people to wear yellow stars.

Source D

In May 1943, after four weeks of heroic resistance, the Jewish uprising in the Warsaw ghetto was finally crushed. What little remained of the ghetto was razed to the ground. Here a Jewish boy is being taken away to a concentration camp.

The extermination of the Jews began after the outbreak of the war. As German tanks rolled east, many Jews were captured in Poland, in the Ukraine and in the Soviet Union. Often whole villages of Jewish people were rounded up and massacred.

Ghettos

Those Jews who survived the initial German conquest were forced to move to special sealed-off areas in towns, called ghettos. The ghettos were run by special Jewish councils, who arranged for food to be distributed and for the children to go to school. But the ghettos were not safe: the Gestapo, Nazi police and the SS raided them regularly, to round people up and take them to their deaths. Sometimes the Jews fought back. When in May 1943 the SS moved into the Warsaw ghetto in Poland, to their surprise the Jews fought back fiercely with guns they had managed to smuggle in. The SS brought up tanks and flame throwers, but still the Jews kept on fighting. The SS were amazed, but in the end they crushed the resistance and sent the last inhabitants of the ghetto to death camps.

Source E

An inhabitant of the Warsaw ghetto gave this eye-witness account:

'We were happy and laughing. When we threw our grenades and saw German blood on the streets of Warsaw, which had been flooded with so much Jewish blood and tears, a great joy possessed us.'

Zivia Lubetkin

Source F

'Amazing! These bandits (Jews) would often rather stay inside burning buildings than be captured by us. And I have seen several leap, on fire, from blazing buildings and thus meet their death. Extraordinary!'

SS Major General Jürgen Stroop, April 1943

The Wannsee Conference and the 'Final Solution'

In January 1942 a group of leading Nazis met in the smart Berlin suburb of Wannsee to decide on a cheap, efficient way of exterminating the Jews of Europe. This Wannsee Conference drew up one of the most frightful plans ever hatched: they decided to wipe out the entire Jewish population using poison gas. Some of the concentration camps would be converted into special extermination camps to carry out the 'Final Solution' to what the Nazis called the 'Jewish Problem'. Within a few weeks the first extermination camp was ready. It was near the Polish town of Oswiecim. The Germans called it Auschwitz.

● Why do you think the Nazis called the plan to exterminate the Jewish race the 'Final Solution'?

Source G

An eye-witness gave this account of a mass execution of Jews in a forest in Poland.

'Without screaming or weeping these people undressed ... [A] father was holding the hand of a boy about 10 years old and speaking to him softly; the boy was fighting his tears. [Nearby there was] a tremendous grave. People were wedged closely together and lying on top of each other so that only their heads were visible. Nearly all had blood running over their shoulders from their heads ... I estimated that it contained about a thousand people. I looked for the man who did the shooting. He was an SS man, who sat at the edge of the pit, his feet dangling into the narrow end of the pit. He had a tommy gun on his knees and was smoking a cigarette.'

Quoted in William Shirer, *The Rise and Fall of the Third Reich*, 1973

The location of concentration camps in Germany and the occupied countries.

Auschwitz

Auschwitz was vast, covering 47 square kilometres (18 square miles). It had a chemicals factory, with a large slave labour camp attached. In 1942 Auschwitz became an extermination camp.

Jews, Gypsies, homosexuals and prisoners of all kinds were sent to Auschwitz from all over Europe. They travelled in cattle trucks, often standing up all the way, with no food or water. Many died on the journey.

When they arrived at Auschwitz, they were immediately sorted into those who could work and those who could not. People who could work were taken away; people who were too old or too ill to work, as well as most of the children, were all sent straight to the gas chambers. Usually, to prevent panic the victims were told they were going to have a shower, and sometimes music played as they went in. At some camps, prisoners were used by SS doctors for scientific experiments.

Source I

Ovens used to burn the bodies of the dead in Belsen concentration camp.

Source H

A French prisoner described how people were gassed at Auschwitz.

'The men stood on one side, the women on the other. They were addressed in a very polite and friendly way: "You have been on a journey. You are dirty. You will take a bath. Get undressed quickly." Towels and soap were handed out, and then suddenly the brutes woke up and showed their true faces: this horde of people, these men and women were driven outside with hard blows and forced both summer and winter to go the few hundred metres to the "Shower Room". ... The doors were shut ... then SS Unterscharführer Moll threw the gas in through a little vent. One could hear fearful screams, but a few moments later there was complete silence.

Twenty to twenty-five minutes later, the doors and windows were opened to ventilate the rooms and the corpses were thrown at once into pits to be burnt. But beforehand the dentists had searched every mouth to pull out the gold teeth. The women were also searched to see if they had not hidden jewellery in the intimate parts of their bodies, and their hair was cut off and methodically placed in sacks for industrial purposes.'

Source J

Auschwitz. Most people arrived here by train, in cattle trucks.

Source K

'As many as twenty-five persons were put at one time into a specially constructed van in which pressure could be increased or decreased as required. The purpose was to find out the effects of high altitude and of rapid parachute descents on human beings. Most of the prisoners who were made use of died as a result of these experiments, from internal haemorrhages of the lungs or the brain.'

Records of the Nuremberg War Trials, 1946

Source L

Fritz Stangl, Commandant of Treblinka, another extermination camp, explains how he felt about his victims.

'**Q**: Would it be true to say that you finally felt the Jews weren't human beings?

A: Cargo. They were cargo. … I remember … the pits full of blue-black corpses. It had nothing to do with humanity – it couldn't have; a mass of rotting flesh. Wirth (a senior SS official) said, "What shall we do with this garbage?" I think that started me thinking of them as cargo.'

1971

Source M

A mass grave for the victims of the Holocaust.

After the war, many Nazis were tried and executed for their part in the Holocaust. Adolf Eichmann was one of the most well-known Nazi war criminals. He helped work out the details of 'the Final Solution', and was present at the Wannsee Conference. From then till the end of the war, it was his job to organise for Jews, especially in Hungary, to be sent to the extermination camps.

After the war he was captured by the Americans but escaped to South America under a false name. In 1960 he was kidnapped by the Israelis and put on trial in Jerusalem. He was hanged in 1962.

Source N

Eichmann told his Israeli interrogator:

'I'm covered with guilt, Herr Hauptmann (Captain), I know that. But I had nothing to do with killing Jews. I've never killed a Jew. And I've never ordered anyone to kill a Jew.'

Jochen von Lang, *Eichmann Interrogated*, 1983

Source O

Adolf Eichmann on trial in Jerusalem.

PORTRAIT OF A NAZI:

ADOLF EICHMANN

EARLY YEARS He came from a large family in Austria. His parents were regular church-goers. Eichmann went to the same secondary school as Hitler. He did not work hard and was taken out of school by his father, who sent him to technical college.

WORK He was an apprentice in an Austrian electrical company for a couple of years, before getting a job as a travelling salesman. In 1933, during the worldwide slump, he was made redundant and went to Germany to look for work.

NAZI PARTY Eichmann joined the Nazi Party and the SS part-time in 1932. When he went to Germany in 1933 he became a full-time member of the SS. He quickly won promotion and became a Lieutenant Colonel.

- It is true that Eichmann never personally murdered anyone. Look back at the events for which he was actually responsible. Was he right when he said
  - he had never killed a Jew
  - he had never ordered anyone to kill a Jew?

---

1 Using information in this unit, construct a time-line showing what the Nazis said and did about Jewish people in the period 1922–45.

2 What evidence is there in this unit to show that some Germans did not consider the Jews to be human beings?

3 Why do you think the Nazis treated the Jews in such an appalling way?

4 Suppose you were the Israeli prosecutor in 1962. What charges could you bring against Eichmann? (*Note*: You must be able to prove the charges.)

18 Bombing

In 1992 a statue of Sir Arthur Harris, the commander of RAF Bomber Command, was unveiled in London. Many people protested, saying that the bombing of civilian targets in Germany was little more than murder. Others said it was vital in winning the war.

What did bombing actually achieve?

Bombing had to be carefully planned. Targets tended to be of four types.

- **Military sites**

  The German Luftwaffe bombed British radar stations and airfields during the Battle of Britain. The RAF bombed the German forces gathering in France to invade Britain, and U-boat bases during the Battle of the Atlantic.

- **Communications**

  Roads, railways and bridges, which the enemy needed in order to move troops, were targets for the bombing.

- **Industry**

  Modern armies need vast stocks of weapons and ammunition. Both sides viewed the factories that provided these supplies as *legitimate* bombing targets.

- **Civilians**

  At the start of the war, each side tried to avoid hitting areas where ordinary people lived, but bombs often missed factories or bridges and hit houses instead. The Germans launched the *Blitz* on British cities; later the Allies bombed German cities even more ferociously.

Getting to the target was difficult because of enemy fighter aircraft and anti-aircraft fire, called *flak*. The only sure defence was to have fighters to escort the bombers, but fighters could only carry enough fuel to fly fairly short distances, so most groups of bombers had to travel on to their targets alone.

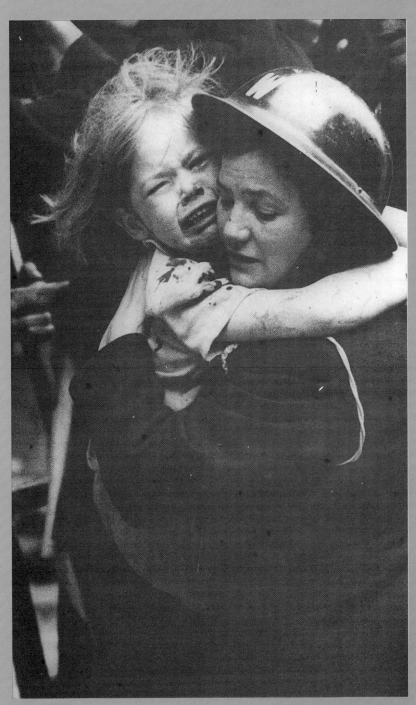

Source A

A little girl is rescued from a bombed building in London.

The Germans bomb Britain

The first heavy bombing began in 1940 during the Battle of Britain. London, Coventry and other British cities were heavily bombed by the Luftwaffe in what was called the Blitz. In Plymouth, the bombing was so fierce that the people nearly rioted, but for the most part bombing merely strengthened people's resolve to fight on.

Source B

'(The raids on Exeter) created a wonderful spirit of comradeship which broke down all the barriers of class in the city … Some people were left with no gas in their homes and couldn't even boil a kettle. They were invited into the homes of neighbours who still had power, to cook their meals.'

Express and Echo, '50th Anniversary of the Blitz', 1992 edition

Source C

'Everybody is worried about the feeling in the East End where there is so much bitterness. It is said that even the King and Queen were booed the other day when they visited the destroyed areas.'

Harold Nicolson, *Diaries and Letters*, entry for 17 September 1940

The big raids on Germany continue. British war plants share with the R.A.F. credit for these giant operations.

THE ATTACK BEGINS IN THE FACTORY

Source D

This poster showing Lancaster bombers attacking a target in Germany gives a vivid picture of a night-time bombing raid. What was the purpose of this poster?

A formation of US B17 bombers on a daylight bombing raid.

Source F

A stricken B17 Flying Fortress over Berlin on a daylight raid. Its tailplane has been mangled by bombs from aircraft higher in the formation. Losses like this happened because bomber formations often contained hundreds of aircraft.

The Allies bomb Germany

The RAF began bombing Germany as soon as the Germans bombed London, and went on bombing until the end of the war. For most of the war, bombing was the only way the British had of actually hitting back at Germany. The bombers aimed mostly at German industrial towns and U-boat bases. Germany was too far away for British fighters to escort the bombers, so the Germans were able to shoot down hundreds of aircraft. Those that did get through often missed their targets. In 1941 more British aircrew were killed than German civilians.

After 1941, the Americans took over bombing in daylight, and the RAF switched to bombing at night. It cost the Americans hundreds of aircraft, but it also meant the Allies could launch massive raids on German cities. A single raid by a thousand bombers destroyed the city of Cologne, and in 1943 the centre of Hamburg was destroyed in four nights of heavy bombing that created a terrible *firestorm*.

Source G

The devastated centre of Dresden.

Dresden

It is estimated that in February 1945 more than 35,000 people were killed in a massive British bombing raid that destroyed the city of Dresden in eastern Germany. Dresden was a particularly beautiful city, with no heavy industry. In February 1945 it was packed with refugees fleeing from the Russians.

There have been many arguments about the Dresden raid.

Was it justified?

1 The Russians wanted a heavy bombing raid on a city to destroy bridges and railway lines. It would also clog up the roads with refugees so that the Germans would not be able to move their troops.

2 The British government Target Committee considered the Russian request, and decided Dresden should be the target. They told Bomber Command to arrange the raid.

3 Dresden was quite unprepared for the raid. The whole of the centre of the city was destroyed, partly by bombs and partly by a massive firestorm.

Source H

One survivor remembers the firestorm.

'I stumbled on towards where it was dark. Suddenly, I saw people again, right in front of me. They scream and gesticulate with their hands, and then to my utter horror and amazement I see how one after the other they simply seem to let themselves drop to the ground. I had a feeling that they were being shot, but my mind could not understand what was really happening. Today I know that these unfortunate people were the victims of lack of oxygen. They fainted and then burnt to cinders. I fall then, stumbling over a fallen woman and as I lie right next to her I see how her clothes are burning away.'

A McKee, *Dresden, 1945: The Devil's Tinderbox*, 1982

Source I

When Churchill began to doubt whether the raid was justified. Harris wrote to him.

> Dear Prime Minister
>
> ### The Dresden Raid
>
> What really makes any sort of (German) recovery almost impossible is ... the complete dislocation of transportation ... You will remember that Dresden was recommended by the Target Committee as a transportation target as well as on other grounds... Attacks on cities ... are strategically justified in so far as they tend to shorten the war and so preserve the lives of Allied soldiers ... I do not personally regard the whole of the remaining cities of Germany as worth the bones of one British Grenadier.
>
> Yours sincerely
> Arthur Harris
> RAF Bomber Command

Source J

Arthur Harris planning the bombing offensive against Germany.

Source K German war production

	1940	1942	1944
Military aircraft	10,200	14,200	39,500
Tanks	1,600	6,300	19,000
Heavy guns	4,400	5,100	24,900

Adapted from Max Hastings, *Bomber Command*, 1979

Source L

A leading Nazi later commented on the impact of bombing.

'We would have been able to keep our promise of delivering forty boats a month by early in 1945, however badly the war was going otherwise, if air raids had not destroyed a third of the submarines at the dockyards.'

Albert Speer speaking in the 1960s, quoted in D. Saward, *Bomber Harris*, 1984

New terror weapons

Towards the end of the war the Germans began to use two new weapons: the V1, a small pilotless aircraft packed with explosives – a flying bomb; and the V2, a giant rocket with an explosive warhead. V stood for *Vergeltung*, retaliation, because British and American bombers had devastated German cities. These weapons did damage London but no worse than the raids during 1940–41. Hitler's scientists were on the point of discovering how to split the atom and might have developed an atom bomb if Germany had not been defeated in 1945.

> A television company has decided to stage a debate on whether the British bombing of German cities was justified. Using the information from this unit, produce a report that can be used in the televised debate, either for or against the bombing. You may wish to mention:
> ● the different types of target
> ● civilian casualties
> ● civilian morale
> ● German attacks on British cities
> ● German war production.

19 D-Day

For three years, most of the fighting against Germany was going on in Russia. Many people began to ask when the British and Americans would open a second front against the Nazis.

Why did it take so long to open the Second Front?

Hitler had built a huge line of defences all along the Atlantic coast, from Denmark to Spain. He called it his Atlantic Wall. The Allies soon learned how strong it was.

In 1942 a large force of Canadian and British troops attacked the French port of Dieppe. The Germans were well prepared and cut the attackers to pieces.

In 1941 and 1942, the Russians did most of the fighting against the German army. They were desperate for the British to attack the Germans in the west, to relieve the pressure, but the British were unable to do this alone. They had to wait for American help.

In 1942 the British were still fighting a difficult battle against Field Marshal Rommel in North Africa. They wanted to finish this campaign before opening any new fronts.

Italy

Instead, Churchill suggested attacking Italy. He thought this would be much easier than an attack on the Germans in France. It turned out to be more difficult than he imagined. The Germans rushed troops into Italy and fought every inch of the way. The Americans and British were soon pinned down in the mountains and the advance seemed to come to a halt.

Planning

By 1944 Churchill was ready to agree to an attack on German-occupied France. The Allies practised on beaches in England. One practice ended in tragedy. As the Americans were coming ashore at Slapton Sands in Devon, two German boats attacked the landing crafts, and hundreds of Americans were drowned. If this had happened on the day of the real invasion it would have been a disaster.

Source A ▼

General Dwight D. Eisenhower, centre, with his council of war. Montgomery is on his left.

Preparing for D-Day

The invasion was code-named *Operation Overlord*. The Supreme Commander for Overlord was the American General Dwight D. Eisenhower. His deputy was the British General Montgomery. The German commander in France was their old enemy from North Africa: Rommel.

Transporting a massive army across the Channel onto a defended beach was not easy, and careful, detailed planning went into Overlord.

1 Where should Eisenhower attack?

The Germans expected the Allies to attack near Calais, where the Channel is very narrow. The Allies bombed the area around Calais, to make the Germans think the attack was coming there. But in fact a surprise attack was planned further west, in Normandy.

2 What were the German defences like?

The Germans had put obstacles on the beaches to tear open the bottoms of any boats that attempted to land. The invasion would be at low tide, when the obstacles would be exposed on the shore.

3 How would the troops deal with the German heavy guns and tanks?

The Allies would be bringing their own tanks and heavy guns with them. Special amphibious tanks were designed which could float ashore, rather like the modern hovercraft. The tanks would lay a track along the beach for vehicles to move on.

4 How could the air force and navy help the invading army?

Before D-Day the Allies would bomb and destroy all the railways, bridges and roads in the invasion area, to stop the Germans bringing in reinforcements.

Also, paratroops would land the night before the invasion and seize all the bridges and crossings that would be needed by the Allies. British minesweepers would clear a way for the invasion fleet. But the biggest question was still:

5 How could troops and supplies be landed safely?

British engineers invented floating harbours – *Mulberries* – which were towed across the Channel.

6 Wouldn't the Germans know the invasion was coming?

Yes, but they would not know *when*, nor exactly *where*. And if the bombing of Calais worked, the Germans would be ready and prepared – but in the wrong place. Nothing was left to chance. The invasion, code-named *D-Day*, was scheduled for early June 1944, but it proved very windy and stormy. The meteorologists forecast a slight break on 6 June. 'OK,' said Eisenhower, 'let's go.'

The Germans were caught completely by surprise. They were still expecting the main attack to be near Calais, and they did not have many troops stationed in Normandy. Even after D-Day, they kept most of their troops near Calais, in case the main attack was still to come there. Now it seemed that nothing would stop the Allies. Winston Churchill and King George VI crossed the Channel to visit the beaches. General de Gaulle, leader of the Free French in exile, rushed over to get back on French soil again. In Normandy itself, people offered the Allied troops wine and danced in the streets as they advanced. But things were not over yet.

Mulberry

At first the Mulberry harbours worked very well, but on 17 June they were wrecked by a storm. The port of Cherbourg was so badly destroyed that when the allies captured it they had to carry on using the Mulberry harbours.

The bocage

The Normandy countryside is criss-crossed by tall, thick hedges, known in French as the *bocage*. The bocage provided excellent cover for the Germans, who fought for every hedge and field. It took the Allies weeks to break through this fierce German resistance.

Caen

The British launched a massive bombardment to force the Germans out of the city of Caen. The Germans surrendered, but Caen was completely destroyed.

The Falaise Gap

The Allies surrounded the Germans in an area around the town of Falaise that became known as the Falaise Gap, and bombed them mercilessly with fighter-bombers. Nearly 10,000 Germans were killed in one of the bloodiest battles of the war.

How the Mulberry Plan worked

A temporary sea wall of scuttled ships and concrete blocks provided shelter for the piers where the ships could dock. The piers stood on adjustable steel legs and were linked to the land by pontoon bridges.

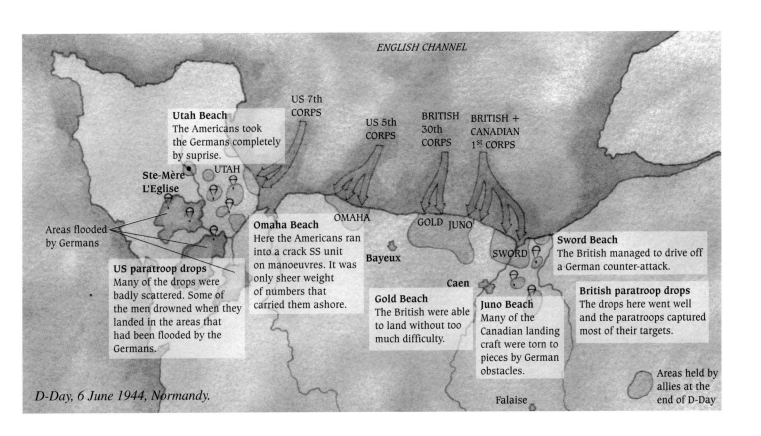

ENGLISH CHANNEL

US 7th
CORPS

US 5th
CORPS

BRITISH
30th
CORPS

BRITISH +
CANADIAN
1st CORPS

Utah Beach
The Americans took the Germans completely by suprise.

Ste-Mère
L'Eglise

UTAH

Areas flooded by Germans

OMAHA

GOLD   JUNO

SWORD

Sword Beach
The British managed to drive off a German counter-attack.

Omaha Beach
Here the Americans ran into a crack SS unit on manoeuvres. It was only sheer weight of numbers that carried them ashore.

Bayeux

Caen

US paratroop drops
Many of the drops were badly scattered. Some of the men drowned when they landed in the areas that had been flooded by the Germans.

Gold Beach
The British were able to land without too much difficulty.

Juno Beach
Many of the Canadian landing craft were torn to pieces by German obstacles.

British paratroop drops
The drops here went well and the paratroops captured most of their targets.

D-Day, 6 June 1944, Normandy.

Falaise

Areas held by allies at the end of D-Day

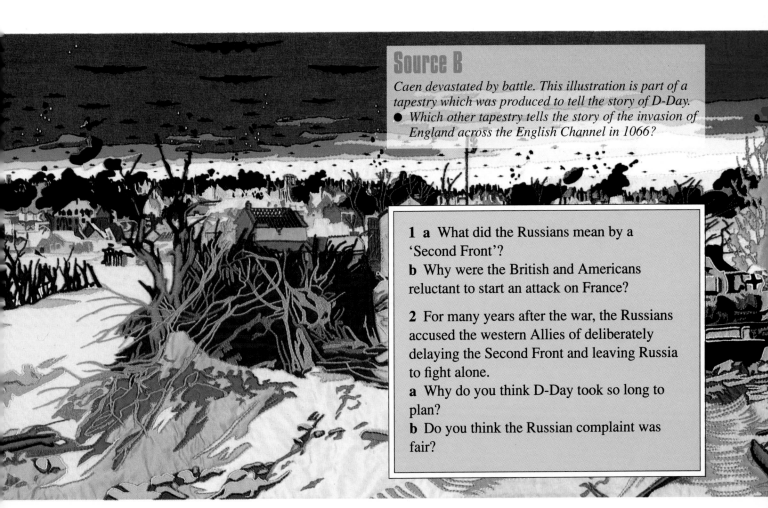

Source B

Caen devastated by battle. This illustration is part of a tapestry which was produced to tell the story of D-Day.
● *Which other tapestry tells the story of the invasion of England across the English Channel in 1066?*

1 a What did the Russians mean by a 'Second Front'?
b Why were the British and Americans reluctant to start an attack on France?

2 For many years after the war, the Russians accused the western Allies of deliberately delaying the Second Front and leaving Russia to fight alone.
a Why do you think D-Day took so long to plan?
b Do you think the Russian complaint was fair?

20 Germany collapses

With the Russians advancing from the east and the British and Americans racing forwards in the west, Hitler was as determined as ever to fight on.

Why did the Germans not surrender sooner?

The Bomb Plot

Part of the answer to this question lies in what happened on 20 July 1944. On that day, Hitler held a conference with some of his generals. One officer, Count von Stauffenberg, was called away to the telephone and left the room, leaving his briefcase behind. The briefcase contained a bomb. No sooner was Stauffenberg out of the room than the bomb went off.

Hitler was incredibly lucky. The thick oak table in the room protected him from the blast, though the others in the room were badly injured and some were killed. But he was badly shaken, and determined to get his revenge.

It soon became clear that many German officers had known about the plot. The SS began to round them up. Colonels, generals, even field marshals were arrested and shot. Others were sentenced to death and immediately taken out to be strangled with piano wire and strung up on meat hooks.

Most of the army were terrified. To stop them surrendering to the Allies, Hitler threatened to shoot the family of any soldier who gave himself up.

In the east, the Germans were only too well aware of the terrible things they had done in Russia. They knew how they had treated Russian prisoners and they were afraid that if they surrendered the Russians would kill them.

The Battle of the Bulge

At Christmas 1944 Hitler launched a massive counter-attack against the Americans in France. The Americans were taken by surprise, and the Germans quickly cut them off. German soldiers disguised as Americans spread confusion behind the American lines. The Germans called on the Americans to surrender, but the American general in command replied, 'Nuts!'

The Germans could not keep up the attack for long. Their tanks ran out of fuel and the Americans were able to push them back. Hitler's last gamble had failed.

Source A
Hitler showing Mussolini the room where he survived the assassination attempt.

The fall of Berlin

Meanwhile, in the east the Russians under Marshal Zhukov were closing in on Berlin. On 25 April 1945, Russian and American troops met up at Torgau, only 120 kilometres from Berlin.

Hitler and his most trusted followers withdrew to a special underground bunker. There he carried on giving orders to a German army that no longer existed. He even took the opportunity to get married to a woman called Eva Braun, and allowed his followers to organise a dance, which was held in the canteen – while overhead Russian soldiers advanced through the streets of Berlin.

Finally, on 30 April 1945, Hitler and his new wife killed themselves. He shot himself through the mouth; Eva swallowed poison.

On 7 May Germany surrendered to the Allies. In Britain and America there was wild rejoicing and dancing in the streets to celebrate VE day – Victory in Europe – on 8 May 1945. People were delighted that finally the war was over.

But it wasn't. In Asia the war with Japan was still going on, and there was every sign that it was getting tougher. It was to be several months more before people in Britain could celebrate VJ day, Victory over Japan, on 15 August 1945.

Source C

A Russian soldier hoists the Soviet flag over the Reichstag building, with the ruins of Berlin in the background.

Source B

American Sherman tanks waiting to go into action in the Ardennes, December 1944.

1 Why do you think the German army fought particularly hard after the Bomb Plot went wrong?

2 What did the Battle of the Bulge show about the German army by the end of 1944?

3 Put the following explanations as to why the Germans did not surrender until 1945 into a rank order of importance.
- Hitler had lost touch with reality.
- The Germans were terrified of the Russians.
- The German army could still fight well.
- Hitler never allowed his generals to surrender.
- The German army was terrified of the SS.

Explain your choice.

21 The atom bomb

In August 1945 the Americans dropped atom bombs on Hiroshima and Nagasaki, and destroyed both cities. There have been furious arguments about this decision ever since.

Why did the Americans decide to drop the atom bombs?

The Manhattan Project

The Allies were terrified that the Germans might construct an atom bomb first. They bombed the German laboratories. The Germans had another problem too. They had forced many of the leading nuclear physicists to flee to Britain or the United States because they were Jewish. Without their help, the Germans could only work slowly, and they still had not made a breakthrough when Germany surrendered in May 1945.

In the United States, Roosevelt gathered together a group of American, Canadian and British scientists, led by an American, Robert Oppenheimer, to work on the atom bomb. It was code-named the *Manhattan Project*.

The scientists worked in secret in a remote village called Los Alamos, in the middle of the New Mexico desert.

In July 1945, the first atom bomb was ready. When the scientists tested it, it left an enormous crater many kilometres wide. The scientists were delighted that the bomb worked, but over-awed at its power. When the bomb went off, Oppenheimer quoted an old Indian poem: 'I am become Death, the destroyer of worlds'.

It was too late to use the bomb on Germany, but the war with Japan was still going on as fiercely as ever. Should the bomb be used there?

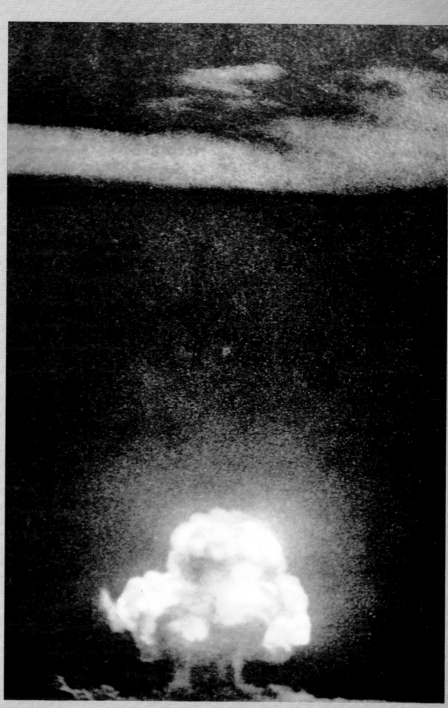

Source A

An atom bomb test explosion, New Mexico, 16 July 1945.

How to defeat Japan

Now that the war with Germany was over, people were impatient to win the war with Japan. But how?

There seemed to be five ways:

1 Invasion

The Japanese were putting up fanatical resistance on the Pacific islands and costing the Americans thousands of casualties. The Americans calculated that invading Japan would cost a million men.

2 Blockade

Japan had no raw materials of its own, and a tight blockade would be a disaster for that country.

3 Bombing

The Americans were bombing Japan heavily. In March 1945 a single raid on Tokyo killed 80,000 people. On the other hand, heavy bombing on its own had not forced either Britain or Germany to give in.

4 Russian help

So far, Stalin had kept out of the Japanese war, but now Germany was dealt with, he became interested in the east. The Russians could attack the Japanese in Manchuria and China. The Americans did not want the Russians to advance that far.

That left one last possibility.

5 Use the atom bomb

But was it right to use it? Even the scientists could not agree.

The man who had to make the decision was the new American President, Harry S Truman.

Dropping the bomb would *definitely*

- kill thousands of Japanese civilians
- give a terrible shock to the Japanese government and people.

Dropping the bomb *might*

- make the Japanese surrender quickly
- save thousands of Allied lives (because now the Allies would not have to invade Japan)
- stop the Russians from advancing too far.

Not dropping the bomb would *probably*

- mean that the Allies would have to invade Japan to force her to surrender.

Not dropping the bomb *might*

- make the war drag on for another year, with further heavy Allied casualties
- give the Russians a chance to advance into China, and possibly even share in the occupation of Japan after the war
- suggest that the Americans were afraid to use it.

Truman decided to use the bomb.

On 6 August 1945, a single US bomber dropped the first atom bomb, nicknamed 'Little Boy', over the Japanese city of Hiroshima. It exploded with a blinding flash. Hiroshima was completely destroyed.

Three days later a second bomber took off. It carried another atom bomb of a different design, nick-named 'Fat Man'. The weather was cloudy, and the pilot could not find his target. He set off instead for his reserve target, the city of Nagasaki. This was where the first Americans had arrived in Japan a hundred years before. 'Fat Man' destroyed the city.

Source C

'Little Boy', the first atom bomb to be used as a weapon, had the power of 20,000 tons of TNT.

Source B

An Allied prisoner of war in Japan said after the war:

'There is no doubt in my mind that these atomic bombs saved many more lives than the tens of thousands that they killed. They saved the lives of tens of thousands of prisoners of war, of hundreds of thousands of Allied Servicemen and almost certainly of millions of Japanese – for, let there be no mistake, if the Emperor and his cabinet had decided to fight on, the Japanese would, literally, have fought to the last man.'

Fletcher-Cooke, *The Emperor's Guest*, 1971

Source D

Allied prisoners of war in a Japanese camp – a painting by Leslie Cole.

Source E

Mr Tanimoto was 3 kilometres away from the centre of the explosion in Hiroshima.

'A tremendous flash of light cut across the sky … Mr Tanimoto threw himself between two big rocks – he felt a sudden pressure and then splinters and pieces of board and fragments of tile fell on him. He heard no roar … Mr Tanimoto met hundreds and hundreds who were fleeing. The eyebrows of some were burned off and slime hung from their faces and hands. Some were vomiting as they walked.'

John Hersey, *Hiroshima*, 1946

Source F

The devastated city of Hiroshima, 6 August, 1945. Between 75,000 and 100,000 people died in the blast. Within five years nearly half a million people died from the radiation effects of the bombing of Hiroshima and Nagasaki.

The Japanese government was in turmoil. Some wanted to carry on fighting, others said it was hopeless. Finally, on 14 August 1945 the Emperor made up his mind. Japan surrendered. The Second World War was over.

Source G

The official surrender of Japan, Tokyo Bay, 2 September 1945 on the quarterdeck of USS Missouri.

Source H

Akihiro Takahashi was at school in Hiroshima in 1945.

'My (school) uniform was blasted to shreds. The skin at the back of my head, my back, both hands and both legs had peeled off and was hanging down like rags.'

BBC, *Children at War*, 1989

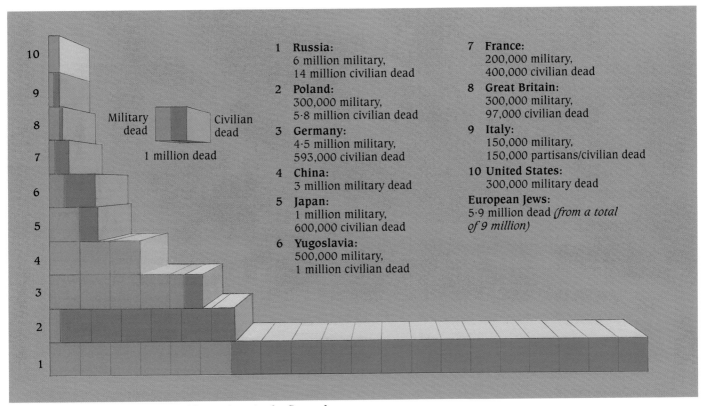

1 **Russia:**
6 million military,
14 million civilian dead

2 **Poland:**
300,000 military,
5·8 million civilian dead

3 **Germany:**
4·5 million military,
593,000 civilian dead

4 **China:**
3 million military dead

5 **Japan:**
1 million military,
600,000 civilian dead

6 **Yugoslavia:**
500,000 military,
1 million civilian dead

7 **France:**
200,000 military,
400,000 civilian dead

8 **Great Britain:**
300,000 military,
97,000 civilian dead

9 **Italy:**
150,000 military,
150,000 partisans/civilian dead

10 **United States:**
300,000 military dead

European Jews:
5·9 million dead *(from a total of 9 million)*

Military dead · Civilian dead
1 million dead

The number of casualties suffered by nations in the Second World War.

Source 1

A jubilant American Serviceman in Piccadilly Circus celebrating the surrender of the Japanese.

1 a What different methods could the Americans have used to defeat Japan?
b For each method, explain its advantages and disadvantages.

2 There were many reasons why President Truman decided to drop the atom bomb. Put these reasons in order, starting with the most important.
◆ The Manhattan Project had cost a lot of money, so it would be a waste not to use the bomb.
◆ Invading Japan would cost too many Allied lives.
◆ No one in America or Britain much cared about how many Japanese were killed.
◆ Blockading Japan would take too long.
◆ Truman wanted to end the war with Japan quickly before the Russians joined in.
◆ A demonstration explosion would have been difficult to arrange and might not have persuaded the Japanese to surrender anyway.

3 a Do you think the Americans were *right* to use the atom bomb? (This is a difficult question to answer. You will need to think about it carefully and weigh all the evidence. Remember that there are very good arguments on both sides.)
b Do you think they needed to drop the *second* bomb?

22 Rebuilding Europe

It is difficult now to imagine the devastation in Europe in 1945. Whole cities were reduced to rubble, and the roads and railways were clogged up with refugees.

How did Europe recover from the war?

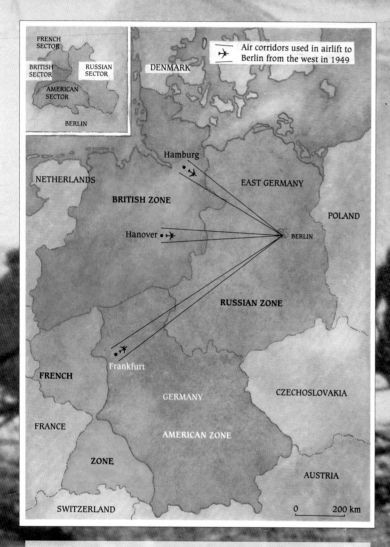

How Germany was divided by the Allies in 1945.

Air corridors used in airlift to Berlin from the west in 1949

Germany

The German government had disappeared, so the Allies had to provide one of their own. Germany and Austria were divided up into four zones governed by the Allies: the USA, the Soviet Union, Britain and France. The two capital cities, Berlin and Vienna, were also divided into four sectors. In their zone, the Russians began dismantling German factories, and sent machines back to Russia. The Americans and British tried to help the Germans rebuild the shattered homes which they themselves had bombed. In all the zones, people in important positions who had supported the Nazis were replaced with anti-Nazis.

Dealing with the Nazis

Hitler, Goebbels and Himmler were all dead, but the Allies managed to capture a number of leading Nazis, including Hermann Göring. These people were charged with war crimes and tried at a special court at Nuremberg. The court watched films from concentration camps, and listened to witnesses. The Nazi leaders all said they were only obeying orders from other people. The court did not believe them, and most of them were sentenced to death.

Source A

People queuing for a bucket of water in devastated Berlin in 1945.

The Marshall Plan

Europe was utterly devastated by the war and desperately needed

- new homes
- new factories
- new railways and roads.

In addition, millions of people had been killed or maimed during the war. The American Secretary of State, General George C. Marshall, offered aid to European countries, as long as it was carefully planned and allocated. Western countries accepted the offer eagerly, but the Russians were suspicious that Marshall Aid was a way of increasing American power in Europe, and refused it. Thanks to Marshall Aid, western Europe recovered much more quickly than the areas under Russian control.

Source B

The Nuremberg Trial. The surviving leaders of the Third Reich were put on trial for war crimes at the Nuremberg law courts. Twelve received the death sentence. The Allies made ordinary Germans come into the concentration camps to see for themselves what had been going on. Many Germans claimed this was the first they had known of the Holocaust.

Refugees

The Nazis had torn people from their families all over Europe and transported them to nearly every part of the continent. There were thousands of people in concentration camps in Germany and Poland. Children had been stolen from their parents and were with new families in Germany. Thousands of people had moved westwards to escape the Russians as they advanced. Not all of the refugees wanted to go home. Many preferred to start a new life in Britain or the United States. Sorting out who all these millions of people were, providing them with food and clothing, and working out where they would go (and where they would be allowed to go) was a huge task. The Red Cross did a lot of the work, and they were helped by a new organisation, the United Nations.

Why do you think the Allies tried the Nazis, instead of leaving it to the German courts?

The end of empires

After 1945, people in Africa and Asia demanded their independence from European rulers. In some cases this was granted peacefully; but in many cases these demands led to war. Newly independent states, such as India and Indonesia, came into existence.

The United Nations

The Allies set up the United Nations Organisation to replace the old League of Nations. Unlike the League, the UN could use troops, as it did in Korea in 1950. But the UN was soon bogged down in disputes between its member states. Some of its best work was to be in non-political fields, like medicine and help for refugees.

Soviet control of Eastern and Central Europe

The Russians put communist governments in power in the eastern and central European countries occupied by Soviet troops during the Second World War. When the people of these countries protested, as they did in East Berlin and Hungary in the 1950s, and in Czechoslovakia in 1968, the Russians sent in soldiers and tanks to crush them.

The Vietnam War

After China became communist in 1949, communist groups staged risings all over Asia. In Vietnam, the USA fought a long and bitter war to stop the communist North Vietnamese taking over South Vietnam. The Americans poured in troops and bombed the Vietnamese heavily but still could not defeat the Vietnamese communists. In 1973, the Americans agreed to pull out of Vietnam, and in 1975 South Vietnam fell to the communists.

Conflict in the Middle East

In 1948 the UN created a new state of Israel in part of Palestine. The Palestinian Arabs resented losing their land. Neighbouring Arab states attacked Israel in a series of wars but the Israelis withstood the Arab onslaught.

The fall of the Berlin Wall

In 1961 the communist government of East Germany built a wall across the centre of Berlin, to stop people escaping to the West. Hundreds of people were shot trying to get over the wall. In the late 1980s, the new Soviet leader, Mikhail Gorbachev, tried to reduce tension with the West. In 1989, with communist governments collapsing all across Eastern Europe, the wall was demolished.

23 The end of empires

After the Second World War, European nations gradually gave the peoples in their overseas empires their independence. Sometimes independence was achieved peacefully; often it was accompanied by bloodshed.

Why was de-colonisation often violent?

India – protests against British rule

The British Empire was called the 'empire on which the sun never sets', because the sun was always shining on at least some part of it. The largest colony in the British Empire was India. Since about 1885, an Indian National Congress had made peaceful protests against British rule. In 1919 British troops under the command of General Dyer opened fire on a peaceful protest meeting in the Sikh city of Amritsar. This resulted in 379 Indians being killed and 1200 injured. There was a wave of protest across India. The leader of the protesters, Mohandas Gandhi, said the British could no longer be trusted.

Gandhi

When the Second World War broke out, Gandhi told his followers to do nothing to help either the British or the Japanese. Gandhi did not believe in using violence. Instead, he preached *satyagraha*, the force of truth. He said that, as long as a cause is a good one, you can achieve it without using force but by non-violent means, such as strikes, demonstrations and boycotts. Gandhi was widely respected for his teaching, and Indians called him the *Mahatma* (Great Soul). The British were worried about the effect his speeches were having on the Indian people, and put him in prison.

Source A

General Dyer faced a Court of Inquiry.

Q: When you got into the square, what did you do?
Dyer: I opened fire.
Q: At once?
Dyer: Immediately I had thought about the matter, and it did not take me more than 30 seconds to make up my mind as to what my duty was …
Q: In firing, was your object to disperse the crowd?
Dyer: Yes.
Q: Any other object?
Dyer: No sir. I was going to fire until they were dispersed.
Q: Did the crowd at once start to disperse as soon as you fired?
Dyer: Immediately.
Q: Did you continue firing?
Dyer: Yes.

India Office Records

Over 2 million Indian soldiers fought for the Allies during the war. Some Indians, however, fought on the Japanese side, hoping it would hasten their independence. But most followed Gandhi's preaching of satyagraha. During the war, the British government agreed to grant independence to India once the war ended, in return for the Indian support of the Allies' cause. Gandhi and the Indian leaders in Congress began a 'Quit India' campaign to persuade the British to go immediately. In 1945 the new Labour government set about the task of granting India independence as soon as possible.

Religious conflict

People of many different religions lived together in India, for example Hindus, Muslims, Sikhs, Buddhists and Christians. The largest group were the Hindus (207 million) followed by the Muslims (62.5 million). Gandhi wanted one united independent India, but the leader of India's Muslims, Mohammed Ali Jinnah, wanted Muslims to have a separate state. Dividing India up in this way was called partition. The man who would have to decide whether or not to partition India, and if so how, was the new Viceroy (the governor acting for the sovereign), Lord Louis Mountbatten.

Source B

After Hong Kong and Singapore were lost to the Japanese, this Indian Nationalist cartoon was published showing a defeated Churchill being driven out of the region. ▼

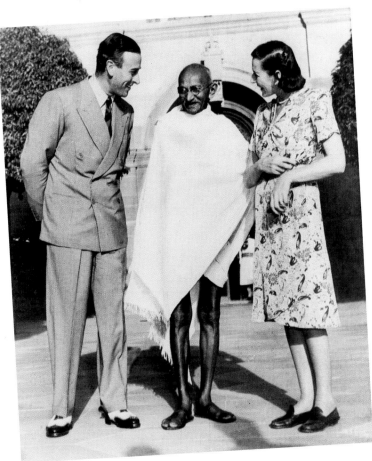

Source C ▲

Lord and Lady Mountbatten with Gandhi.

117

MOUNTBATTEN'S PROBLEM

1. Timing

It is now February 1947. The British government has promised India her independence by June 1948. Will that be:

- long enough to reach a decision about partition
- too long, and encourage impatient Indians to get violent?

2. If India is partitioned

- Where will the border be between the Hindu state and the Muslim state?

- What happens to people living on the 'wrong' side of the new borders?

3. If India is kept united

- Will it not just make for trouble if Hindus and Muslims are forced to live together in one state?

Mountbatten made two decisions:

Decision 1
Britain will pull out of India in August 1947 – eleven months ahead of schedule.

Decision 2
India will be partitioned into a Hindu state, India, and a Muslim state, Pakistan.

Source D

Dead bodies being cleared away from the streets of Calcutta after rioting between Hindus and Muslims.

Source E

A train travelling from Delhi to Lahore carrying Muslim refugees after partition in 1947.

Source F

Gandhi wrote about his ideas in the magazine *Young India*.

'My non-co-operation is rooted not in hatred but in love. I cannot love Muslims and Hindus and hate Englishmen. Where there is love, there is life. Hatred leads to destruction.'

Gandhi, 1920s

Source G

During partition, appalling massacres were carried out.

'I remember an officer's wife arriving by train. The train had been stopped outside Chaklala and she heard shrieks and groans (the time was just about dawn). She lowered a shutter, and looked out, to find Sikhs being dragged out of the carriages and hacked to pieces by the side of the line. She was horrified and screamed, whereupon one of the band came up to her carriage and said, "Don't be frightened, Memsahib, nobody will harm you. We've got this job to do, and then the train will go on."'

General Sir Frank Messervy, 1963

Partition

British rule in India ended on 15 August 1947, but thousands of Indians now found themselves living in the 'wrong' country, and had to travel hundreds of kilometres to reach the 'right' one. Millions of Sikhs in the Punjab felt they belonged to neither. On the way, there were scenes of appalling violence, particularly between Muslims and Hindus. Some Hindus wanted India to attack Pakistan and take it back. Although he was old and ill, Gandhi repeatedly went on hunger strike to stop the fighting. It helped to calm the violence, but it did not heal the hatred between Muslims and Hindus. Some Hindus even blamed Gandhi for allowing the Muslims to set up their own state and, on 30 January 1948, one of these Hindus shot Gandhi dead while he was at prayer.

119

Algeria and the FLN

The North African state of Algeria was ruled by France. It had a large population of French settlers. Some of the Algerian nationalists formed the FLN (*Front de la Libération Nationale* – National Liberation Front) to force the French to leave. Unlike Gandhi, the FLN firmly believed in using violence. So did the French.

By 1957, the FLN and the French settlers were each shooting and bombing each other without mercy. The FLN planted a bomb in a milk-bar used by French mothers and children and in a café full of students dancing to music from a juke box. The French army responded by using torture on any FLN suspect they caught.

Source H

One FLN leader defended the bomb in the milk-bar and the café.

'I see hardly any difference between the girl who places a bomb in the milk-bar and the French aviator who bombards a mechta [village].'

Alistair Horne, *A Savage War and Peace*, 1987

Source I

Muslim demonstrators unfurling their FLN flags in front of French police in Algeria.

Source J

Torture was used to get FLN suspects to talk.

'The first of the tortures consisted of suspending the two men completely naked by their feet, their hands bound behind their backs, and plunging the heads for a long time into a bucket of water to make them talk. The second torture consisted of suspending them, their hands and feet tied behind their backs, this time with their heads upwards. Underneath them was placed a trestle, and they were made to swing, by fist blows, in such a fashion that their sexual parts rubbed against the very sharp pointed bar of the trestle.'

Alistair Horne, *A Savage War and Peace*, 1987

The OAS

In 1961, the new French President, General de Gaulle, decided to grant Algeria her independence. The French settlers were upset and furious. They left Algeria and returned to France, where they continued to oppose de Gaulle. Many joined the OAS (*Organisation de l'Armée Secrète* – Secret Army Organisation), a terrorist group set up by rebel French generals. The OAS planted bombs in Paris and tried to assassinate de Gaulle, but the plot failed. The OAS leaders either fled or were imprisoned.

Source K

A French OAS poster.

The Congo

The Congo, in central Africa, was a Belgian colony until it became independent in 1960. The Belgian authorities had done very little to prepare the people of the Congo for independence. Within days, there were riots against the whites still living there; at the same time, the rich southern province of Katanga declared itself independent, and the Congolese army murdered the Prime Minister. The country fell into chaos.

The United Nations sent troops into the Congo to try to keep the various groups apart. The UN troops also helped the Congolese to defeat the rebels in Katanga. Three years later the Congo changed its name to Zaire.

There were furious arguments in the United Nations about the situation in the Congo. The Russians accused the UN of taking sides in the war instead of simply trying to keep the peace.

The Bandung Conference

In 1955, President Sukarno of Indonesia, newly independent of the Dutch, hosted a conference of leaders from African and Asian countries, either free of European rule or hoping to be.

As more countries achieved their independence, they began to talk of themselves as the 'Third World', or as the 'non-aligned' countries, separate from the big power-blocs of Russia and America.

Source M

An extract from President Sukarno's speech at the Bandung Conference.

'Sisters and brothers! How terrifically dynamic is our time! ... We, the people of Asia and Africa ... far more than half the human population of the world, we can mobilise what I have called the Moral Violence of Nations in favour of peace.'

Source N

President Sukarno on an official visit to Pakistan, in 1963.

Source L

Indian United Nations troops capture two white mercenaries in the Congo, in January 1963.

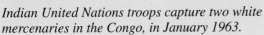

1 Who was Gandhi? What were his beliefs? Did other people in India agree with Gandhi?

2 Explain in your own words why Lord Mountbatten had to decide about partitioning India. If you had been there, what would you have advised him to do?

3 Read the section on Algeria carefully. Do you agree with the writer of Source H? Give your reasons.

4 Using information from this unit, explain why there was widespread bloodshed when some countries became independent.

24 Communist China

In 1949, China emerged from years of confusing and bloody civil war to become the world's second communist superpower. Led by Mao Tse-tung, the communists changed many aspects of life in China.

What was the impact of the communist take-over?

At the start of the twentieth century, China was still ruled by an Emperor. The Chinese government was corrupt and hopelessly inefficient. China's millions of peasants were at the mercy of landlords who set high rents and took away everything belonging to tenants who could not afford to pay them. Women were treated as servants and, in some areas, it was common practice to kill girl babies at birth.

In 1911 the Emperor was overthrown and a republic was set up under Dr Sun Yat-sen. Within a year, he was forced to resign and China fell into the hands of ruthless regional warlords. For the next ten years, China was in complete chaos.

The Kuomintang and the communists

Two groups wanted to take control in China.

The Kuomintang
● The *Kuomintang* was Sun Yat-sen's party and had a large army led by General Chiang Kai-shek.

The communists
● The Chinese Communist Party was founded in 1921. Its leader was Mao Tse-tung.

Sun Yat-sen wanted to work with the communists against the warlords, but Chiang Kai-shek did not trust the communists. In 1925 Sun died and Chiang took over the Kuomintang. Chiang suddenly turned against the communists, and had thousands of them murdered.

Source A

Chiang Kai-shek (left) with Dr Sun Yat-sen, the first president of the Republic of China, in 1923.

Source B

The Chinese communists wore red neck-scarves, which left a tell-tale red stain:

'I myself saw a rickshaw stopped, the coolie grabbed by the police, his shirt jerked from his neck disclosing the red stain ... He was rushed to the side of the road, compelled to kneel down, and unceremoniously shot while the crowd of people in the street applauded.'

R. North, *Chinese Communism*

The Long March

Even when the Japanese invaded Manchuria in 1931, Chiang concentrated on attacking Mao. In 1934, Mao had to lead his men on a long retreat westward, then northwards, to escape the Kuomintang. This became known as the Long March.

The Long March was extremely hard for the communists. Much of the land they crossed was wild and rugged and the Kuomintang attacked them ceaselessly, killing 80,000 of them. Unlike the Kuomintang and the warlords, Mao gave strict orders that his men should treat the peasants fairly. Eventually Mao reached Shansi Province in northern China and made it a communist state.

Source C ▼

Mao Tse-tung and some of his soldiers on the Long March.

Source D

Mao's rules for his troops on the Long March.

1. Be polite and courteous to everyone at all times.
2. Return anything you borrow.
3. Replace anything you damage.
4. Don't cheat the peasants.
5. Pay for everything you need.

Source E

A painting by Liu Lun of the capture of Luting Bridge. Mao's men managed to defend themselves and to escape from ▼ *Chiang Kai-shek's army.*

The Cultural Revolution

In 1957 Mao invited people to say honestly and openly what they thought about the way he ruled China. 'Let a hundred flowers bloom', he said; but when people started criticising him he quickly changed his mind and imprisoned his critics. In 1966 Mao took offence at a play about a loyal official who is sacked unfairly by the Emperor – Mao thought the Emperor was meant to be him. He decided to launch a new Cultural Revolution and use the students to protect his revolution.

Source F

Mao proclaiming the People's Republic of China in 1949.

The communist revolution

During the Second World War, Mao and Chiang both fought against the Japanese. After the war, the Kuomintang proved as corrupt and inefficient as ever. Inflation was so bad that shops weighed paper money instead of counting it. Support for Chiang crumbled. In 1948 Mao decided to try to turn Chiang out. The communists took Peking (Beijing), then Nanking and Shanghai a few months later. Chiang fled to the island of Formosa (Taiwan) with his supporters. The next year, in October 1949, Mao announced that the country was now a communist state – the People's Republic of China.

Changes on the land

Mao realised that no revolution could succeed in China without the support of the peasants. Landlords were arrested by the peasants who had once worked for them and put on trial in People's Courts. Most were either shot instantly or sentenced to hard labour. In 1956 Mao introduced collective farms, arranging villages into communes, where livestock and equipment were held in common. Unlike Stalin, Mao allowed peasants to keep small plots of land for themselves.

In 1958, Mao announced a Five-Year Plan to industrialise China, called the Great Leap Forward. It was a disaster. It was hopelessly ill-planned, and the government had to lie desperately about the results to make it look successful.

In 1966 thousands of students and young people joined a new organisation called the Red Guards and were encouraged to stage vast parades in praise of Mao. Millions of Chinese bought the pocket-sized book of the *Thoughts of Chairman Mao*, known as his 'Little Red Book', and everyone took care to study it – especially in public. Schools were closed for a time and town dwellers and intellectuals forced into the country to work on farms. The Red Guards roamed around looking for anything Western or 'anti-revolutionary' which they could attack. They began arresting and beating up doctors, teachers, even Communist Party officials – anyone who was educated enough to think for themselves. The victims were publicly humiliated for not being revolutionary enough, put before courts and made to confess to crimes they had not committed. Some 400,000 people were murdered in this way by the Red Guards. The Chinese Prime Minister, Lui Shao-chi, was arrested and left to die, naked, in a police cell.

Source G
Students reading Mao's 'Little Red Book'.

Source H
A parade in support of Mao Tse-tung.

125

Source I

Jung Chang was at school in China when the Cultural Revolution broke out. In this extract she describes what happened.

'In practically every school in China, teachers were abused and beaten, sometimes fatally. Some schoolchildren set up prisons in which teachers were tortured … A wave of beating and torture swept the country, mainly during house raids. Almost invariably, the families would be ordered to kneel on the floor and kow-tow to the Red Guards; they were then beaten with the brass buckles of the Guards' leather belts. They were kicked around, and one side of their head was shaved, a humiliating style called the "yin and yang head", because it resembled the classic Chinese symbol of a dark side (*yin*) and a light side (*yang*). Most of their possessions were either smashed or taken away.'

Jung Chang, *Wild Swans*, 1991

Source J

Red Guards singing revolutionary songs on a march to Beijing.

After Mao

Eventually Mao agreed to wind the Cultural Revolution down. By the time he died in 1976, the moderate communists, led by Deng Xiao-ping, were back in control. Mao's widow, Chiang ching, and three others, together nicknamed the Gang of Four, wanted a new Cultural Revolution. They were arrested, publicly humiliated and jailed, as people who had spoken against them in the same way during the Cultural Revolution had been. But Deng Xiao-ping was not prepared to introduce democracy. In 1989 Chinese students staged a sit-in in Tiananmen Square in Beijing and demanded democratic government. The government sent tanks into the square, and the students' leaders were arrested. Many of the protesters were killed by the army.

Source K

A lorry carrying students on their way to demonstrate for democracy in Tiananmen Square in 1989.

Source L

Soldiers and tanks in Tiananmen Square after the students' demonstration had been crushed.

1 What was the Kuomintang? Why did the Kuomintang and the communists fight each other?

2 What was the Long March? How did it help Mao to take power in China?

3 Read Source I. How does it help us to understand what the Cultural Revolution was like?

4 Read this unit carefully. Do you think the evidence suggests that life in China changed a great deal during the twentieth century?

25 Post-war America

The United States was the wealthiest and most powerful country in the world after the Second World War. Despite its wealth and power, the USA was in many ways a divided society.

What divisions existed in post-war America?

Source A

Glamorous 1950s advertisements designed to appeal to Americans with money to spend.

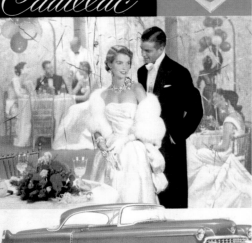

Maybe This Will Be The Year!

During the 1950s, much of the world was still slowly recovering from the effects of the war. In the United States, however, many people could afford to buy cars, washing machines, refrigerators, even foreign holidays, on easy terms, paying by instalments. Smart new suburbs sprang up outside America's cities. By the 1960s, the USA produced nearly half of all the cars in the world, and three-quarters of the world's steel. Despite this, however, in some areas of America, people still lived in desperate poverty.

Senator McCarthy

In 1950, Senator Joseph McCarthy of Wisconsin claimed that he had a list of over 200 leading communists working in the American government. Ordinary Americans were horrified: they were terrified of communism, and were very pleased when McCarthy led a US Congressional Committee to find out who was a communist and who was not. McCarthy did not only call government officials before his committee. Writers, trade unionists, army officers, even Hollywood film stars appeared before him. McCarthy was a bully and forced witnesses to inform on other people. Much, though not all, of McCarthy's evidence was made up, and in the end his committee was closed down. Some innocent people had their lives destroyed and were not able to work in America again.

Source B

Senator McCarthy with newspaper headlines exposing a spy scandal in Britain in 1951. Scandals like these gave him more fuel for his anti-communist campaign in the USA.

The struggle for civil rights for black people

The southern states of America had passed special laws that forced black people to live separately from white people. Black people could not sit where they liked on buses, nor shop where they liked, and had to send their children to separate black schools. In 1954 the US Supreme Court said that it was against the law to stop black children from going to the same schools as white children, but most white people and even the police in the south took no notice. In 1957 President Eisenhower ordered troops to be sent into Little Rock High School, in Arkansas, to protect black students from the whites who wanted to stop them going to the school.

Source E

Martin Luther King addressing the civil-rights rally at the Lincoln Memorial in Washington, DC.

Source C

White women shout insults at Elizabeth Eckford as she tries to enter Little Rock High School through the lines of National Guardsmen.

Source D

Elizabeth Eckford describes her first day trying to go to Little Rock High School:

'I saw a large crowd of people standing across the street from the soldiers guarding Central High School ... The crowd was quiet. I guess they were waiting to see what was going to happen. When I was able to steady my knees, I walked up to the guard who had let the white students in. When I tried to squeeze past him, he raised his bayonet and the other guards closed in and they raised their bayonets. They glared at me with a very mean look and I was very frightened and didn't know what to do. I turned round and the crowd came toward me ... shouting, "No nigger bitch is going to get in our school! Get out of here!".'

Daisy Bates, *The Long Shadow of Little Rock*, 1962

Source F

Martin Luther King spoke to a huge rally at the Lincoln Memorial in Washington DC, in August 1963.

'I have a dream that one day this nation will rise up and live out the true meaning of its creed: We hold these truths to be self-evident, that all men are created equal. I have a dream that one day on the red hills of Georgia the sons of former slaves and the sons of former slave owners will be able to sit down together at the table of brotherhood ... I have a dream that my four little children one day will live in a nation where they will not be judged by the colour of their skin, but by the content of their character.'

In Montgomery, Alabama, Mrs Rosa Parks, a black woman, sat in the 'whites only' section on a bus and was arrested. In protest, the black people of Montgomery staged a massive boycott of the bus company. In the end the bus company was forced to allow black people to sit where they pleased.

These black protests were led by Dr Martin Luther King. He told black people they should campaign for the same civil rights as white people, but they should do so without using violence. Dr King won immense respect around the world, and he was awarded the Nobel Prize for Peace. However, in 1967, he was shot dead by a white extremist.

Young America

Many American teenagers in the 1950s had more money than ever before and a growing sense of independence. Rock and roll music became popular. Teenagers wore jeans and casual clothes, very different in style from those their parents had worn. By the 1960s, young Americans had a pop culture of their own. Bright casual clothes and long 'hippie' hair styles became fashionable.

Source H

Following the assassination of President Kennedy, a judge administers the oath of office to President Johnson on board an aircraft. Mrs Kennedy is to the right of the new President.

In particular, he planned to improve the position of American blacks.

In 1963, he was assassinated in Dallas by Lee Harvey Oswald. To this day there are endless theories about whether or not Oswald was acting on his own or as part of a wider conspiracy.

Source G

A publicity shot of Elvis Presley from the 1950s.

President Kennedy

When the young John F. Kennedy was elected President in 1960, many Americans saw him as a symbol of hope for the future. A Democrat like Roosevelt, he saw the need to help those Americans who had not shared in the wealth of the post-war years. He tried to help the American poor with government money and food.

1 Who was McCarthy? Why do you think so many Americans supported his hunt for communists?

2 Explain in your own words why Elizabeth Eckford (Source D) needed soldiers to help her go to school. Why do you think the soldiers are also hostile to her?

3 What evidence can you find in this unit to show that the USA was a divided society in the years after the Second World War?

26 | The Cold War

After the ending of the Second World War, the governments of the USA and the USSR became more and more suspicious of each others' motives. Each side armed for a war which was feared, but which never came. This long period of hostility was known as the Cold War, and did not finally end until the late 1980s.

Who won the Cold War?

The birth of the Cold War

The Cold War began almost as soon as the Second World War ended. The Russians refused to allow free elections in the countries they controlled in Eastern Europe, or to allow those countries to accept Marshall Aid. Gradually they made sure that communist groups took over the governments of Eastern Europe. Winston Churchill declared in 1946 that an 'Iron Curtain' had fallen across Europe, cutting the free countries of the West off from the Soviet Empire in the East.

East and West distrusted each other and prepared for a possible war. In 1947, the US President, Harry Truman, declared that the USA would help anyone who was fighting against a communist take-over. This policy became known as the Truman Doctrine.

Source A

President Harry Truman in his office at the White House.

Source B

In 1947 US President Harry Truman announced the Truman Doctrine:

'I believe that it must be the policy of the United States to support free peoples who are resisting attempted subjugation by armed minorities or by outside pressures.'

The Cold War

1945	Potsdam Conference. The Allies fall out.
1946	Churchill attacks the 'Iron Curtain'.
1948	The Soviet Union blockades Berlin.
1949	Western Allies form Nato. Communist revolution in China.
1950	War in Korea
1953	Peace in Korea. East German government crushes revolt in Berlin.
1955	Soviet Allies form the Warsaw Pact.
1956	Soviet tanks crush an anti-Russian rising in Hungary.
1960	A US spy plane is shot down over the USSR.
1961	East Germans build the Berlin Wall.
1962	Cuban Missile Crisis
1968	The Vietnam War is at its height. The Soviet Union invades Czechoslovakia.
1972	US President Nixon visits China.
1979	The Soviet Union invades Afghanistan.
1989	Revolutions topple communist regimes in Eastern Europe.

End of the Cold War

ICELAND

UNITED STATES, CANADA

NORWAY
SWEDEN
FINLAND

DENMARK

USSR

EIRE

UNITED
KINGDOM

NETHERLANDS

EAST
GERMANY

POLAND

BELGIUM

Countries joining the
Warsaw Pact

Countries joining NATO

FRANCE

WEST
GERMANY

CZECHOSLOVAKIA

SWITZERLAND

AUSTRIA

HUNGARY

ITALY

ROMANIA

YUGOSLAVIA
(Communist but neutral)

PORTUGAL

SPAIN

BULGARIA

ALBANIA

GREECE

TURKEY

Europe during the Cold War. In 1949, the West set up the North Atlantic Treaty Organisation (NATO). In 1955, the Soviet Union and its allies joined together in the Warsaw Pact.

The Berlin airlift

Germany was at the heart of the Cold War. At the end of the Second World War it was occupied by the victorious Allies and divided into four zones, British, French, American and Russian. Berlin was deep inside the Russian zone but it, too, was divided into four sectors between the Allies. In 1948, the British, French and Americans joined their zones of Germany and sectors of Berlin together, to make a West German state. With American money, West Germany was much better off than East Germany. This was particularly obvious in Berlin, where Berliners in the Russian sector could see the way the western half of the city was flourishing. In 1948, the Russians decided to cut off all West Berlin's land links with the outside world. The Allies were to be starved out of West Berlin and then the Russians would take it over.

The Western Allies replied with a massive airlift of supplies. Everything the people of West Berlin needed – food, clothes, medicines, even children's toys – was brought in by planes flying in an endless relay. It was dangerous: 79 men were killed in flying accidents during the airlift. But it worked. Stalin lifted the blockade.

Source C

German children watch an American cargo plane land at Tempelhof Airport, in Berlin, during the blockade which lasted from 26 June 1948 to 12 May 1949.

132

Korea

In 1950 attention suddenly shifted eastwards. The communist government in North Korea invaded South Korea. The South Koreans appealed to the UN for help. The UN agreed to send an army to help them.

The UN army was mainly American, although it contained troops from Britain and over 14 other countries. Its commander was an American hero from the Second World War, General Douglas MacArthur. MacArthur pushed the North Koreans back over the border fairly easily but then, to the alarm of some of America's allies, he pressed on into North Korea itself. The Chinese leader, Mao Tse-tung, did not want MacArthur to conquer North Korea. In October 1950, he sent half-a-million Chinese troops into Korea to drive MacArthur back.

The Chinese drove MacArthur out of North Korea and invaded the South. MacArthur called on President Truman to use nuclear weapons against the Chinese. There were protests at this among America's allies, as well as within America itself. Truman sacked MacArthur. The new UN commander, US General Omar Bradley, managed to push the Chinese back into North Korea. After a ceasefire was agreed in 1953, both sides were separated by a de-militarised zone which stretched more or less along the original border.

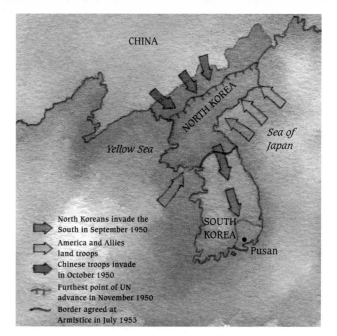

North Koreans invade the South in September 1950

America and Allies land troops

Chinese troops invade in October 1950

Furthest point of UN advance in November 1950

Border agreed at Armistice in July 1953

Korea after the 1953 ceasefire.

Source F

President Truman with General MacArthur in 1950. After his dismissal, General MacArthur returned to a hero's welcome from the Americans, who were stirred up by McCarthy's campaign against communists.

Source D

A young American factory worker describes the reactions among his friends when the Korean War broke out:

'They had a problem over there. We wanted to do something about it. And I guess I didn't have a lot to do at home. We started preaching around the town, saying, "Come down to the Albany! Join the service!". I remember driving one kid of seventeen home to his parents to sign the papers.'

Bill Patterson, speaking in 1985

Source E

American soldiers and their tanks with the UN forces in Korea.

Spies and bombs

The whole of 1949 was a tense period for governments in the West: not only did Mao Tse-tung seize control of China, but the Russians declared that they too had the secret of the atomic bomb. Western scientists raced ahead to make the even bigger hydrogen bomb, but the Russians soon declared that they had the secret for that too. How had the Russians caught up so quickly?

The answer seemed to be that there were a number of Russian spies operating in the West. These were not just Russians, but Westerners sympathetic to communism.

Those shown below were not the only ones. It is easy to see why so many people supported Senator McCarthy's hunt for communists; it is also easy to see why spy stories became so popular during the Cold War.

Julius and Ethel Rosenberg.

Spies operating in the West

Klaus Fuchs.

1950

Name	Dr Klaus Fuchs
Nationality	Originally German Naturalised British
Occupation	Physicist
Activity	Passed secrets about the atomic bomb to the Soviet Union
Sentence	Prison

1951

Names	Julius and Ethel Rosenberg
Nationality	American
Occupations	Civil servant (Julius Rosenberg) Housewife and singer (Ethel Rosenberg)
Activity	Arranged for information about the hydrogen bomb to be passed to the Soviet Union
Sentence	Death by electric chair

1951

Names	Guy Burgess and Donald MacLean
Nationality	British
Occupation	Diplomats
Activity	Operated as Soviet agents inside the British Foreign Office
Sentence	Escaped to Moscow before they could be caught and put on trial

Guy Burgess in Moscow in 1957.

The Soviet hold on Eastern Europe

The Soviet Union ruled Eastern Europe harshly. Anyone who criticised Soviet control was sent to a labour camp. There was no freedom of speech. In 1953, the Russians crushed a rising in East Berlin. Three years later they turned against Hungary.

In 1956, a new Hungarian government took office, led by Imre Nagy. Nagy was a communist, but he wanted to free Hungary from Russian control and to have contact with the West. When he took Hungary out of Russia's alliance system, the Warsaw Pact, the Russians sent tanks in to overthrow Nagy and put in a leader who would be more loyal to Moscow. Nagy was hanged by the Russians.

◢ Source G

Hungarian freedom fighters burnt all the Soviet literature they could find on the cobblestones in front of this building, and then cut out the communist star from the centre of the Hungarian flag.

▽ Source H

One of the 2,500 Soviet tanks that moved in to Hungary in November 1956. After ten days of bitter fighting, the freedom fighters were completely crushed. Russian tanks remained on the streets.

The Berlin Wall

Meanwhile, in Germany thousands of people were escaping from the East through West Berlin. In 1961, the East German government took a drastic step to stop them. A high wall was constructed around West Berlin, cutting it off completely from communist East Germany. Until the wall was demolished in 1989, hundreds of people were killed trying to cross it.

Czechoslovakia

In 1968, it was the turn of the Czechs. The Czech leader, Alexander Dubček, tried to allow more freedom of speech, and started releasing people who had been arrested by the secret police. Even though Dubček stressed that he was still a loyal communist, that did not save him. In 1968 the Russians sent tanks into Prague to overthrow Dubček's government and bring Czechoslovakia into line.

Source J

Ordinary people defied the Russian tanks in Prague as best they could.

Source I

Alexander Dubček.

Source K

Rocket launchers on parade in Red Square on May Day 1956.

Nuclear confrontation

Each side had formed alliances, just as countries hostile to each other had done before the First World War. Europe was divided between the countries who had joined NATO and the Soviet Union and its allies, who had formed the Warsaw Pact.

Both sides began stockpiling nuclear weapons; at first, nuclear bombs, later, by 1960, intercontinental ballistic missiles (ICBMs). Unlike bombs, which need to be dropped from aircraft, ICBMs can be fired directly at targets many thousands of kilometres away. They can also be carried close to their targets by submarine. But would governments ever actually fire them? In 1962 the world seemed about to find out.

Other communist regimes could also take tough action: the Romanian and East German secret police were notoriously ruthless. In the early 1980s, the Bulgarian secret service assassinated an anti-communist Bulgarian broadcaster, in London, in broad daylight, using poison concealed in the tip of an umbrella. In 1981, the Polish government used its army to clamp down on the trade union movement, Solidarity, whose members had been protesting against communist rule.

136

The Cuban Missile Crisis

The Caribbean island of Cuba had been virtually controlled by America until there was a communist revolution in 1959. Cuba's new leader, Fidel Castro, took over all the American businesses on the island. In October 1962, American spy planes reported that nuclear missile sites were under construction on Cuba. The missile sites were Russian, and the missiles were aimed at the United States.

The US President, John Kennedy, decided to act fast. He did not want the Russians to base nuclear missiles so close to the United States; on the other hand, if he pushed the Russians too far, there could be a worldwide nuclear war.

The Cuban missile crisis

22 October President Kennedy announces a naval blockade of Cuba.

24 October Russian ships carrying missiles towards Cuba halt in mid-ocean.

26 October Soviet leader Nikita Khrushchev writes to Kennedy offering to remove the missiles if Kennedy promises not to invade Cuba.

27 October Khrushchev sends a second letter. This time he offers to remove the missiles if Kennedy will remove the missiles in Turkey, which the Americans had placed there in early 1962.

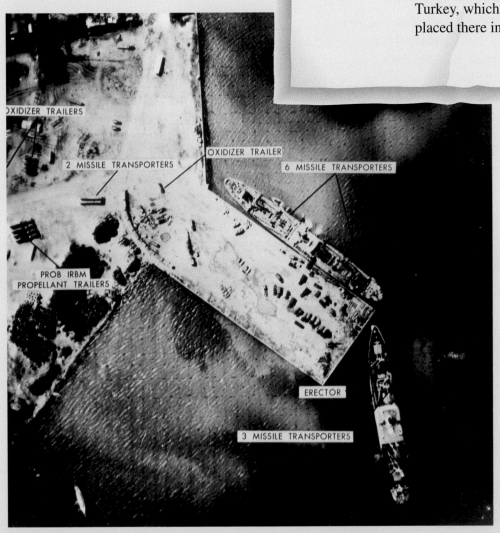

Although American military chiefs wanted Kennedy to bomb Cuba, Kennedy decided to meet Khrushchev half-way. He agreed to the terms in Khrushchev's first letter and simply ignored the second letter. Khrushchev ordered the missiles to be dismantled, and the world breathed again.

Source L
Missile sites at Mariel Port on the island of Cuba in 1962.

137

The end of the Cold War

The Cuban Missile Crisis frightened both sides. In the years that followed, the Americans became bogged down in a long war in Vietnam. The Russians quarrelled with the Chinese and consequently found themselves facing two powerful enemies. By the 1970s both sides were prepared to talk about limiting their stocks of arms, but neither side really trusted the other. In 1979 the Russians invaded Afghanistan and the new American President, Ronald Reagan, stepped up the production of nuclear missiles. He even started spending heavily on weapons in space. The Russians simply could not afford to keep up.

Balance of Nuclear Weapons in 1974

	USA	USSR
ICBMs	1,054	1,575
Submarine-based missiles	656	720
Long-range bombers	437	140

The new Soviet leader from 1985, Mikhail Gorbachev, wanted to modernise the Soviet Union, and to do that he had to stop the high levels of spending on arms. He met Reagan three times, and they agreed on big reductions in arms. In 1989 Gorbachev met Reagan's successor, President Bush, and the two men formally agreed to end the Cold War. What followed surprised everyone.

1989: Year of Revolutions

June	The Polish communists are badly beaten in free elections.
September	Hungary pulls down its border barriers with the West.
October	Widespread anti-communist demonstrations take place in East Germany.
November	The East German government opens up the Berlin Wall. Communist governments in Czechoslovakia and Bulgaria collapse.
December	The communist government in Romania is overthrown.

Source M

Mikhail Gorbachev talks with Ronald Reagan in the White House, during his 1987 visit to the USA.

Two years later, in 1991, communist rule in the Soviet Union itself collapsed. The Cold War was over.

1 How did the Cold War begin?

2 Explain what happened in:
  ● the Berlin Airlift
  ● the Korean War
  ● the Cuban Missile Crisis.
  Which side do you think 'won' in each case?

3 What happened in:
  ● Berlin in 1953
  ● Hungary in 1956
  ● Berlin in 1961
  ● Czechoslovakia in 1968?
  Who do you think 'won' in each case?

4 Using all the information in this unit, say who you think won the Cold War and why.

27 The Vietnam War

In the 1960s, the United States became involved in a long war against the communist state of North Vietnam. Eventually the Americans were forced to admit that they had failed to defeat the Vietnamese communists.

Why did the Americans become involved in this war, and why did they lose?

Vietnam is in Southeast Asia. It was a French colony until the Japanese took it during the Second World War. When the French returned in 1945, they found that the Vietnamese communists, led by Ho Chi Minh, controlled the northern half of the country. In 1954 the Vietnamese communists surrounded and defeated a large French force at the Battle of Dien Bien Phu. The French pulled out, leaving North Vietnam in the hands of Ho Chi Minh. South Vietnam became a separate state, led by President Ngo Dinh Diem.

The Americans were alarmed by the French defeat at Dien Bien Phu. They believed in what was called the Domino theory. This stated that if one country in Southeast Asia fell to the communists, all its neighbours would follow, like a row of dominoes. Because of this, the Americans supported President Diem's government in South Vietnam.

Then, in 1964, came a bolt from the blue.

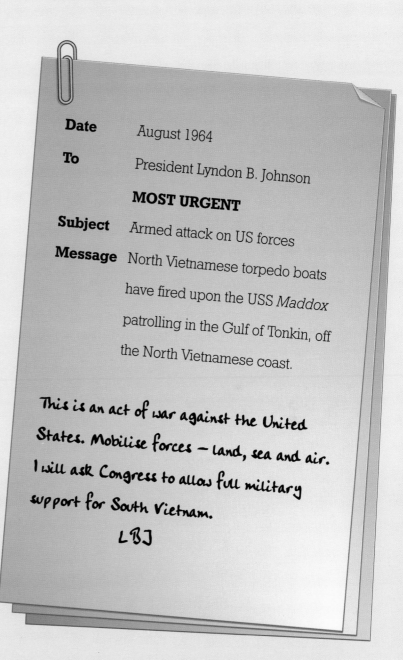

Date   August 1964

To   President Lyndon B. Johnson

MOST URGENT

Subject   Armed attack on US forces

Message   North Vietnamese torpedo boats have fired upon the USS *Maddox* patrolling in the Gulf of Tonkin, off the North Vietnamese coast.

This is an act of war against the United States. Mobilise forces — land, sea and air. I will ask Congress to allow full military support for South Vietnam.

LBJ

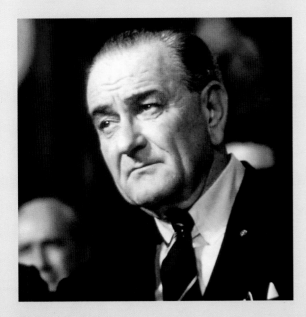

Source A

The US President, Lyndon B. Johnson.

Congress agreed to military intervention, and Johnson poured men and equipment into South Vietnam. Australia and New Zealand, Thailand and South Korea also sent some troops.

The next year, in 1965, the Americans began Operation Rolling Thunder – massive bombing of military targets in North Vietnam. Despite overwhelming American power in the air, American generals were soon telling Johnson that this was not going to be a short or an easy war.

Source B

A US B-52 bomber dropping bombs on the North Vietnamese capital, Hanoi, in 1966.

Date January 1966
To President Lyndon B. Johnson

THE PROBLEM

We are fighting TWO enemies:
1. The North Vietnamese Army (NVA)
2. South Vietnamese communists, or Viet Cong (VC)

Our bombers can hit NVA bases, but VC bases tend to be hidden away in dense jungle. Also, the VC are South Vietnamese, so it is difficult to tell them apart from the ordinary villagers we are supposed to be protecting.

We can EITHER

● use the air force to bomb VC bases in the jungle (We have more than enough bombers to do it, and we can drop napalm – a jellified petrol that burns fiercely – and agent orange – a chemical that destroys vegetation – to strip the jungle bare, BUT in the Second World War bombing only made people more determined to resist.)

OR we can

● use helicopters to send troops deep into the jungle on 'Search and Destroy' missions against VC bases. (The difficulty will be telling the difference between VC bases and ordinary villages.)

OK, we'll use both methods.

LBJ

The American attacks were successful against the NVA, but North Vietnam sent supplies to the Viet Cong along the Ho Chi Minh Trail. The Americans bombed the trail heavily, but they could never stop the supplies getting through. The North Vietnamese dug hundreds of individual bomb shelters, which made it easier to survive bombing raids, and they replaced bombed bridges with bamboo bridges which could be lowered into the water to fool American reconnaissance cameras.

Many ordinary Vietnamese were angry with the corrupt government of South Vietnam. To make matters worse, some American soldiers took out their frustration on ordinary Vietnamese, whether or not they were in the Viet Cong. Gradually, the North Vietnamese and the Viet Cong were winning the battle for the hearts and minds of the ordinary Vietnamese.

Vietnam and the Ho Chi Minh Trail.

Source C

US Marines in a 'Search and Destroy' mission.

Protests in America

In America, many young people protested against the war. When draft cards – the cards calling young men up to join the army – started arriving, many young men burned them or fled to Canada. Even so, President Johnson's popularity rating leapt by 14 per cent when he started bombing North Vietnam. What probably turned most Americans against the war was seeing close-up news coverage on television of some of the savage fighting going on in Vietnam.

Source D

This front-page photograph was taken from television news footage of the execution of a Viet Cong suspect.

Source E

An American soldier describes how he felt about going to Vietnam:

'I wanted to go to war. It was a test that I wanted to pass. It was a manhood test, no question about it. I did not know then the way I know now how safe my life had been. But some part of me knew that Vietnam was the event of my generation.'

Peter Riddick *Vietnam: the Controversial War*

Source F

Crowds protesting daily outside the White House taunted President Johnson (LBJ) with the chant:

'Hey! Hey! LBJ!
How many kids did you kill today?'

I WANT OUT

Source G

An American anti-Vietnam poster based on the famous recruiting poster for the First World War.

The Tet offensive

During the religious festival of *Tet*, in 1968, the VC and NVA launched a combined and carefully planned, surprise attack on the Americans: they suddenly rose up at points all over South Vietnam, deep behind the American lines. They took the American Embassy in the centre of Saigon, and dozens of public buildings all over the country. For a time it seemed as if they had overrun the whole of South Vietnam.

The Americans and South Vietnamese fought back and drove the VC and NVA out. The North Vietnamese were so badly shaken that they offered to start peace talks. But the news coverage on American television made it look as if the VC and NVA could attack anywhere they liked and as if America simply could not win the war A presidential election was to take place in 1968, and a weary and depressed President Johnson announced that he would be standing down. He had had enough.

142

US General Maxwell Taylor complained of how television presentation could distort what actually happened in the Tet offensive:

'The picture of a few houses, presented by a gloomy-voiced television reporter as an example of the destruction caused in Saigon, created the inevitable impression that this was what it was like in all or most of the city.'

My Lai

Many American soldiers found the fighting in Vietnam bewildering and frustrating, and they often took out their feelings on the innocent Vietnamese. There were many atrocities committed by both sides. One of the worst happened in 1968.

An American patrol under Lieutenant William Calley went out of control in the village of My Lai, and gunned down anyone they saw. There are different estimates of how many they killed: some say about 200, others about 500, and some go as high as 700.

Calley was the only man tried for the killings. He was sentenced to death, but he only served three days in prison and three years under house arrest. He was finally released by President Nixon.

The My Lai case came as a tremendous shock to the Americans. The mother of one of the soldiers at My Lai complained in the *New York Times*, 'I sent them a good boy, and they made him a murderer'.

Source I

Bodies of women and children on the road from My Lai in 1968.

The end of the war

Richard Nixon won the 1968 election, and he was determined to pull America out of the war without actually surrendering.

Nixon's plan

Stage 1 Vietnamisation
American troops begin to withdraw and to hand over to the South Vietnamese forces.

Stage 2 Peace talks
Nixon's Secretary of State, Henry Kissinger, started negotiating seriously for a way out. At the same time, Nixon got on better terms with North Vietnam's main supporter, China.

Stage 3 Bombing
Nixon started bombing even more heavily, even bombing communist bases in neighbouring Cambodia, in order to force the North Vietnamese to come to terms quickly.

In 1973, the United States and North Vietnam finally signed a peace agreement in Paris. Both the USA and North Vietnam pulled all their forces out of South Vietnam.

Source J

Nixon with Chairman Mao in China in 1972.

Source K

US helicopters airlifting embassy staff out of Vietnam in 1975 were besieged by hundreds of South Vietnamese hoping to leave Saigon before the arrival of the NVA.

The settlement only lasted two years. In 1975, the NVA invaded South Vietnam again. With no American forces to stop them, the NVA soldiers reached Saigon easily. There were desperate scenes of panic at the American Embassy, as hundreds of Vietnamese tried to climb on board American helicopters airlifting embassy staff to safety.

Things were even worse in neighbouring Cambodia. The communist *Khymer Rouge* took the capital, Phnom Penh, just as the NVA was taking Saigon. The Khymer Rouge leader, Pol Pot, immediately began imposing his idea of a people's revolution in Cambodia which involved the slaughter of millions of Cambodians. It was only in 1979 that the Vietnamese invaded Cambodia and overthrew Pol Pot's appalling regime.

> **1** Explain in your own words why the USA became involved in the Vietnam War.
>
> **2** What happened in the Tet offensive and at My Lai? Why were they both so disastrous for the Americans?
>
> **3** Explain how President Nixon managed to bring the war to an end.
>
> **4** Why did the Americans lose the Vietnam War? Use this unit to identify as many reasons as you can.

28 Post-war Britain

Britain had dominated the world in the nineteenth century and, at the end of the Second World War, Britain still seemed a powerful nation.

Did Britain enter a period of decline after 1945?

The Beveridge Report

Although Britain played a major role in the Second World War, a large section of its population were still poor and often unhealthy. During the war there had been a widespread feeling that, once the fighting was over, the lives of ordinary people would be improved. The wartime government commissioned Sir William Beveridge to write a report on how to make life better for the British people. It quickly became a best seller.

Beveridge Report 1942

Five 'giants' must be beaten
- poverty
- disease
- ignorance
- squalor
- idleness.

The government must provide
- financial help to combat poverty
- free health care to combat disease
- free education to combat ignorance
- cheap housing to combat squalor
- employment to combat idleness.

All political parties promised to implement the recommendations after the war. In the General Election of 1945, the British people, wanting change, deserted Churchill and the Conservative Party and voted in large numbers for the Labour Party. This was led by Clement Attlee. The new Labour government set about putting the Beveridge Report into practice.

Education

In 1944 the wartime government had passed an Education Act which said, for the first time, that all children should go on to a secondary school.

Health

In 1948 the new Labour government introduced the National Health Service, offering free, basic health care for everyone. This was to be paid for by a new National Insurance Scheme.

Industry

The Labour government nationalised key industries like coal mines, electricity, gas and steel. These industries were run by people appointed by the government and taxes provided money to enable them to modernise.

Source A

A family pose outside their new prefabricated house. After the war there was a tremendous shortage of housing. Many bombed-out families still living in slums were given these houses to rent. Known as prefabs, they were surprisingly popular and people lived in them for many years.

Post-war shortages

People were far from happy in the late 1940s. The government had to continue the rationing of food and clothes and was even forced to introduce bread rationing. Bread had not been rationed during the war. When the new National Coal Board could not provide enough coal for people in the severe winter of 1946–47, many people blamed the Labour government. In 1951, the government organised a huge festival of arts and technology in London. This, and the coronation of Elizabeth II in 1953, helped to lighten people's mood.

The Suez crisis

An international dispute in 1956 showed that Britain was no longer a superpower and could not act without the support of the United States. The Suez Canal runs through Egypt, but it belonged to a private company that was controlled by the governments of Britain and France. In 1956 President Nasser of Egypt nationalised the canal. The British Prime Minister, Anthony Eden, along with France and Israel, sent troops into Egypt to get the canal back.

Source B

Ships at Port Said, sunk by President Nasser's government to block the entrance to the Suez Canal.

Source C

The Conservative Party had been re-elected in 1951. Anthony Eden (above) became Prime Minister in 1955 after Winston Churchill retired.

Suez caused a bitter argument in Britain. Eden's supporters said:

- Nasser had no right to take over a canal that did not belong to him.
- Nasser was behaving like Hitler in the 1930s and had to be stopped.
- Britain and France were still world powers, and should not allow themselves to be humiliated by a small country like Egypt.

Eden's critics said:

- Nasser had every right to take over a canal in his own country and Eden was simply trying to bully him.
- Disputes like this should be settled through the United Nations, and not by force.
- Britain and France were not strong enough to take this sort of action on their own any more.

The Russians supported Nasser and even hinted at a nuclear attack on London. The US President Eisenhower told Britain and France he would cut off American economic aid if they did not pull out of Suez. So Britain and France withdrew.

Immigration

In the 1950s, large numbers of immigrants began arriving in Britain, particularly from the West Indies and India and Pakistan. Some companies, like London Transport, advertised in West Indian newspapers to encourage people to come over and work for them. Some people made the new arrivals welcome, others demonstrated racist attitudes.

Source D

One West Indian came to Britain from Barbados in 1956. He describes what he found:

'My first home in England was a house in Notting Hill Gate shared with about 30 other people, with only one bath and toilet between us. The conditions were appalling, and it cost me £3 a week in rent … The racist exploitation of West Indians was to be seen everywhere. There were signs saying "No Coloureds Please" on various advertisements for flats. As a result, our choice of where to live was extremely limited … Most of us were only allowed to do portering or cleaning jobs in stores or hospitals.'

Claude Ramsay

Unemployment and inflation in Britain

Year	Unemployment (% of total work-force)	Price index
1945	1.2	55
1950	1.5	68
1955	1.2	89
1960	1.7	101.6
1965	1.5	120.8
1970	2.6	151.1
1975	3.9	278.7
1978	5.7	407.2

Source E

A group of young immigrants at Victoria Station in 1958.

THE 'SWINGING' SIXTIES

Source G

The Beatles had a huge impact on Britain. Not only did their records sell but young people copied their clothes, hair style and way of life. London became a world centre for pop music and young fashions.

Source F

The England captain, Bobby Moore, with the English team after they won the World Cup at Wembley in 1966, by beating West Germany 4–2 in the final.

Northern Ireland

In 1968, violence broke out between Catholics and Protestants in Northern Ireland. The Protestants were fiercely loyal to the United Kingdom, but many Catholics wanted Northern Ireland to be part of the Republic of Ireland. The government sent troops in to end the crisis. The troops were intended to stay for a few months. Three decades later, the British Army was still present on the streets of Northern Ireland.

Source H

A burning car on a Belfast street in 1988.

Source I

Striking miners on a picket line outside a coal depot in London, in 1972.

Thatcher's Britain

The Conservative Party, led by Margaret Thatcher, won the 1979 election and immediately brought in many changes. She was the first woman to be the British Prime Minister. She encouraged people to start up their own businesses and to take out loans to buy their own homes. She privatised most of the industries that Attlee had nationalised and severely limited the power of the trade unions.

Strikes

In 1973, during the Conservative government of Edward Heath, the trade unions showed how powerful they had become. A miners' strike cut coal supplies to electricity power stations. This meant that people had to use emergency lighting and candles for several days each week. During the Labour government that followed, the unions took on the government again, objecting to a wage freeze. A series of strikes followed.

Source J

Margaret Thatcher during the 1987 General Election campaign, when she won a third term in office.

1 What was the Beveridge Report?

2 How does the Suez Crisis show that Britain was no longer a superpower?

3 Do you think Britain declined after 1945?

29 The Arab–Israeli conflict

The Jewish state of Israel was founded in 1948. It was immediately attacked by several neighbouring Arab states. Conflict over Israel has continued ever since.

Why has the Middle East been in almost permanent crisis?

The state of Israel

After the First World War, the League of Nations gave Britain trusteeship of much of the former Turkish Empire in the Middle East, including the Arab land of Palestine. To the Jewish people, Palestine is their ancient Promised Land, and they began emigrating there in the late-nineteenth century. Jewish migration increased in the twentieth century especially after the rise to power of Adolf Hitler in Germany. Jewish immigrants wanted to turn Palestine into a Jewish state of their own. News of the Holocaust in Europe made the Jews of Palestine even more determined to create a refuge for Jews in the Middle East.

Jewish militants were unhappy at the attitude of the British authorities, who had to consider both Jews and Palestinians. In 1944 groups of Jewish fighters began a campaign of violence to force the British out. Two years later, Jewish terrorists blew up the British military headquarters in the King David Hotel, killing 91 people. In 1947 Britain decided to hand the whole area over to the United Nations. The UN proposed that Palestine should be divided into a Jewish and an Arab state. The new Jewish state, Israel, was founded a year later. The first Prime Minister of Israel was David Ben-Gurion.

Thousands of Arabs who lived in Palestine were forced to leave their homes. They moved to refugee camps in neighbouring Arab states and the area of Palestine that remained outside Israeli control. From the moment the state of Israel was proclaimed, the Palestinians and the Arab states were its sworn enemies.

Source A

An Israeli officer, Yitzhak Rabin, later Prime Minister of Israel, describes how the Palestinian Arabs were to be dealt with.

'We walked outside, Ben-Gurion accompanying us. A senior Israeli army officer repeated the question: "What is to be done with the (Arab) population?" BG (Ben-Gurion) waved his hand with a gesture which said, "Drive them out."'

Quoted in M. Bleaney and R. Lawless, *The Middle East since 1945*, 1989

Source B

A Palestinian woman describes what it was like to arrive in Jordan as a refugee:

'We arrived in Amman (the capital of Jordan) as street beggars, we knocked at people's doors … They sent us to a camp at Gerash and gave us bread, just throwing it at us, so it was good luck to them that caught it, and the devil take the rest … One day, after about two months, the winter came, all of a sudden, with torrential rain and even snow, and it all came through into the tent and one of my children, the youngest, died of cold in the snow and the mud.'

Major events: 1948-73

1948-49

Arab-Israeli War
Together, the Arab states all attacked Israel. The Israeli army defeated them and extended Israel's own borders.

1956

Suez Crisis
During the Suez Crisis, Israel, Britain and France attacked Egypt until the Americans forced them to withdraw.

1967

Six-Day War
Egypt and Syria threatened to attack Israel, but the Israelis attacked first, capturing Sinai, the Gaza Strip, the Golan Heights and the West Bank of the River Jordan. The Israelis immediately began building Jewish settlements in these areas.

1973

The Yom Kippur War
The Egyptians and Syrians launched a surprise attack on the Jewish holy day of *Yom Kippur*. The Israelis were caught by surprise. Although the Israelis successfully fought back, many people in Israel were shocked by the war.

1973

Oil embargo
At the end of the 1973 war, the Arab countries reduced oil exports to the West. This hit the West very seriously: there were immediate petrol shortages, and oil prices rocketed all round the world.

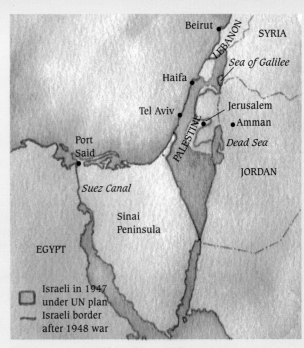

Territory occupied by the Israelis after the 1948-49 war.

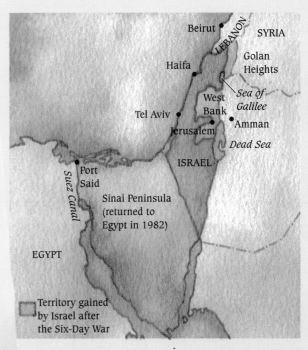

Territory occupied by the Israelis after the Six-Day War.

Source C
Israeli troops pass a burnt-out tank during the Yom Kippur War.

The Palestine Liberation Organisation

At first, Palestinian Arabs looked to other Arab states for help against Israel. After the failure of the Arab armies in a series of wars against Israel, the Palestinians became convinced that they needed to fight for themselves. A number of Palestinian armed groups were set up. These were co-ordinated by the Palestine Liberation Organisation (PLO), which began to use violence against Israeli targets around the world. In 1972, PLO members kidnapped the Israeli team at the Munich Olympics and killed twelve athletes.

The PLO had many supporters, especially among countries opposed to the USA. In 1974, the PLO chairman, Yasser Arafat, persuaded the United Nations to agree that the Palestinians had a right to an independent homeland.

Source D

A PLO terrorist hijacked a British airliner in 1970. Afterwards she justified what she had done in these words:

'(Israel) is in no position to ... accuse me of air piracy and hijacking when (Israel) has hijacked me and my people out of our land. My deed cannot be judged without examining the underlying causes.'

Leila Kaled

Solving the conflict was never going to be easy, because the different groups all distrusted each other. In 1977, President Anwar Sadat of Egypt visited Israel and addressed the Israeli parliament, the *Knesset*. Two years later, he met the Israeli Prime Minister, Menachem Begin, and signed a peace agreement at Camp David in the USA. The PLO and the other Arab states bitterly opposed the agreement, and in 1981 President Sadat was assassinated by his own guards.

Source E

The airliner hijacked by a group of terrorists in 1970 was blown up on the airfield.

Lebanon and the Intifada

In 1975 a bitter civil war broke out in Lebanon. There were PLO bases in Lebanon, and PLO fighters became entangled in the civil war. In 1982 Israel invaded Lebanon to drive the PLO out. The PLO leadership left Lebanon but Israel became caught up in Lebanese politics and was attacked by Islamic fighters.

In 1988 young Palestinians in Gaza and the West Bank began an uprising, the *Intifada*, attacking Israeli soldiers and police with stones or home-made weapons. Their struggle won much sympathy across the world. The PLO leaders used the sympathy created by the Intifada to support their calls for a Palestinian state. Yasser Arafat won important support from America by publicly renouncing the use of violence and accepting that the state of Israel had a right to exist. The USA put pressure on Israel, and in 1993 the Israelis and the Palestinians signed a historic peace agreement. This enabled the PLO to take control of some areas of Gaza and the West Bank.

Source G

An armed Israeli soldier chases away Palestinian women and children who are demonstrating against the Israeli occupation of Lebanon.

1 Explain in your own words how Israel came into existence in 1948.

2 Using all the information in this unit, say why you think it has taken so long to get peace in the Middle East.

30 A new Europe

After 1945 Europe was split in two by the Cold War. Since 1989 there has been talk of a new united Europe.

Is the new Europe really so different from the old?

The European Economic Community

The French and Germans both needed to rebuild their economies after the Second World War, and they also wanted to build better relations between their two countries. The French Foreign Minister, Robert Schuman, suggested that France and West Germany should trade freely in the two most important materials for rebuilding – coal and steel. In 1952, together with Italy, Belgium, Luxembourg and the Netherlands they created the European Coal and Steel Community. Later, in the 1958 Treaty of Rome, these states set up the European Economic Community (EEC), agreeing to abolish customs duties between member states on a whole range of goods. Later, the EEC changed its name to the European Union (EU).

Britain, with several other European countries, formed another organisation, called the European Free Trade Association (EFTA), in 1960. However, the EEC was so successful that the British government applied to join in 1963. The French President,

Source B

Chancellor Konrad Adenauer.

Source A

The German Chancellor between 1949 and 1963, Konrad Adenauer, describes how Robert Schuman proposed his plan for coal and steel:

'In France there was a fear that once Germany had recovered, she would attack France. He could imagine that the corresponding fears might be present in Germany. Rearmament always showed first an increased production of coal, iron and steel. If an organisation such as he was proposing were to be set up, it would enable each country to detect the first signs of rearmament, and would have an extraordinarily calming effect in France.'

Konrad Adenauer, *Memoirs 1945–53*, 1966

General de Gaulle, twice vetoed Britain's application – in 1963 and 1967. De Gaulle believed that Britain was not totally committed to Europe, and would be too easily influenced by America. It was not until after de Gaulle's death that Britain was able to join the EEC in 1973, with Denmark and Ireland. Subsequently Greece joined in 1981, Spain and Portugal in 1986, and Austria, Finland and Sweden in 1994.

The EEC (now the EU) tries to support industry and agriculture in its member states. It provides money to help the poorer regions; it also lays down rules for fishing and farming. There has been a lot of criticism of the EU's Common Agricultural Policy, because some feel that it gives out large sums of money to keep inefficient farmers in business, and sometimes encourages the production of far more of certain types of food than is needed.

The Maastricht Treaty

The Maastricht Treaty, which was intended to strengthen co-operation between members of the EU, was finally signed in 1993. It provoked a lot of argument among ordinary people in Europe. There was strong opposition to it in Britain, Denmark and France; but others thought it was the only way forward for Europe to survive in world markets.

The main points of the Maastricht Treaty were:

- The European Parliament should have more power.

- All members of the EU should prepare for a single European currency.

- EU members should move closer together, to operate more as a single, unified state.

Post-war Europe.

Source C

Inside the European Parliament building in Strasbourg. Member states elect representatives to the parliament every five years.

After 1989: a new Europe?

In 1989, the communist regimes of Eastern Europe collapsed, and the Berlin Wall was pulled down. The leaders of East and West Germany immediately started talking about reunification, and on 3 October 1990 the two parts of Germany were reunited for the first time since the war.

Elsewhere in Europe, old nations began to re-emerge. The different peoples of the Soviet Union set up their own republics, and the Czechs and Slovaks set up separate states. The different peoples of Yugoslavia began to declare themselves independent too. European leaders began to speak of a 'new Europe'.

156

EU members

Former Communist countries that have applied for EU membership

Source E

Officials from East and West Germany meet through a gap in the Berlin Wall.

Source D

Crowds gather along the Berlin Wall in 1989.

Source F

A Polish woman watched the crowds celebrating German reunification:

'I saw them on television, singing that national anthem of theirs beside the Berlin Wall, and I knew we were in for trouble. Poor Poland: we can't get our land back from the Russians, and now the Germans will start demanding Silesia (part of Poland) back from us. I remember 1939. You wait: it's all going to start again.'

John Simpson, *Despatches from the Barricades*, 1990

Source G

Neo-Nazis demonstrate against minority groups in Dresden in 1992.

This new Europe soon showed it had a lot of old problems. In Germany and other parts of Europe, Neo-Nazi groups appeared and began attacking minority groups. In Bosnia, the Serbs, Croats and Muslims began a long and bloody civil war for territory. Atrocities were committed by all sides. The Bosnian Serbs, for example, set up concentration camps and carried out mass executions to clear non-Serbs out of areas in which they wanted to settle. This policy is called 'ethnic cleansing'. The First World War began in Bosnia; by the 1990s, it looked as if the twentieth century had come full circle.

Source H

These words 'Turks out' were painted by Neo-Nazi supporters. Turkish immigrants in Germany are often a target. In 1992, a woman and two girls died after Neo-Nazis set fire to their house.

158